WOMEN ON THE LAND

WOMEN ON THE LAND

Their Story During Two World Wars

CAROL TWINCH

The Lutterworth Press
Cambridge

The Lutterworth Press
P. O. Box 60
Cambridge CB1 2NT

British Library Cataloguing in Publication Data
Twinch, Carol
   Women of the land: their story during the two World Wars
   1. Great Britain. Agricultural industries. Women
   Personnel. Organisations: Women's Land Army, history
   I. Title
   331.4830941

ISBN 0-7188-2814-3

First Published by The Lutterworth Press 1990

Printed in Great Britain by
Billing & Sons Ltd, Worcester

Contents

Illustrations

Preface

In Britain until the middle of the Nineteenth century the work carried out by women on the land was of a traditional nature. Conventionally regarded as light, it largely comprised seasonal tasks like hop-picking or the stooking and binding of sheaves at harvest time, dairying and poultry-rearing - the latter being an enterprise which even well into this century was seen as a woman's province rather than part of the farm business. Only in parts of Scotland were 'bondager' women obliged, until as late as the 1880s, to take on the heavier labouring tasks by virtue of being the sisters, wives, or daughters of farm workers.

A gradually perceived need for social reform in the cities was also to bring about reforms in the countryside, although at a slower pace. As a result of the findings of a Royal Commission set up in 1867, child labour was curbed, and the Gangs Act of 1869 required a licensed 'gangmistress' to accompany the newly segregated female-only gangs. If the establishment, in 1865, of the first Women's Suffrage society had little immediate effect upon women generally, or country women in particular, it did indicate the logical direction of reform.

Towards the end of the century a new class of educated women began to interest themselves in horticulture and agriculture and with places for women at the existing agricultural colleges practically non-existent, the demand was to be met by wealthy private patrons. In 1889, Arthur Harper Bond established Swanley Horticultural College, and Francis Evelyn, Countess of Warwick, bought two large houses in Reading which, in 1898, were used to found Studley College, an agricultural and horticultural college solely for women. Later, in 1904, Viscountess Wolseley started the Glynde School for Lady Gardeners.

For the educated woman, such training might lead to paid employment as gardeners or market gardeners; a teaching position in a rural school; even joining organised co-operative societies, with the chance of finding work in the Dominions. More usually, it meant returning home to oversee the work of the home garden or the home dairy. Such women, in any case, were exceptional, viewed in relation to the great majority, whose aspirations were limited both by education and class.

Then, with the coming of war in 1914, thousands of women from comparatively ordinary backgrounds were suddenly required to go far beyond the old boundaries of dairying and gardening into a hitherto male-dominated world of heavy horses, ploughing, and field work. Women unused to labouring, or even to country life, were called upon to help maintain vital food supplies for the nation. Hundreds of untrained women were to venture further, to work in the woods and forests, felling timber to provide pit props for the mines, as well as working in the huge and dangerous sawmills.

The conditions under which the women volunteers lived and worked were often far removed from those to which they were used, and they had also to contend with resentful male farm workers who viewed them as 'blackleg' labour. Nevertheless, they were to make a demonstrable contribution to British agriculture in those years: from a situation in which, at the outbreak of war, Britain was importing nearly fifty per cent of its total food requirements, by 1918, and despite poor harvests and crop failures, she was producing some eighty per cent of her food. Then, during the Second World War, more than 200,000 women were to follow the lead set by the women of the previous generation and join the new Women's Land Army, while thousands more were to make their contribution through the offices of the National Federation of Women's Institutes, the National Union of Townswomen's Guilds, and the Women's Farm and Garden Association. There were, of course, many women already working in agriculture and in horticulture whose contribution to the national effort should not be forgotten; what was exceptional about the women from the towns was that at the time they volunteered few had any idea about farming or of what they were letting themselves in for!

Women on the Land is essentially the story of how untrained women, from many different backgrounds, coped with food production when Britain was at war. It is a story of courage and of the dauntless acceptance of a farmworker's or forester's way of life.

In writing this book, the pride which the women took in their achievements has shone through, and some to this day have retained a close affinity for farming. It is clear that for many, those years opened up an entirely new way of life, an opportunity to do something completely out of the run of their normal lives. For some it represented a time of growing up, and of acquiring the self-confidence to cope with the tough realities of the world in which they found themselves; for others, their time on the land simply offered adventure.

Due to the fragmentary recruitment and administration of women's farm labour in wartime, there are no archives, as such, for either of the Women's Land Armies. The material selected for deposit in the Public Record Office, indispensible in the search for information, is contained not only among the records of the Board [later Ministry] of Agriculture, and the Ministry of National Service, but also among the less accessible material relating to emergency (and therefore temporary) government departments. There is no mention, for example, of the work of the Women's Timber Corps in the normal Forestry Commission Annual Reports, as the now-defunct Ministry of Supply had overall control. Even within the official channels of research there are numerous dead ends. For instance, a large proportion both of Land Army and Timber Corps members were empoloyed privately and details of these were never logged.

The four moves that the 1939 Women's Land Army undertook between London and Balcombe Place account for yet more gaps. On her first arrival at Balcombe the Chief Administrative Officer was horrified to discover that an involuntary paper trail of master index cards had been laid through the suburbs of London from one of the removal vans. They were never recovered. For the duration of the war the incident touched a raw nerve in the Enrolments Department at HQ, and too-close enquiries were coldly discouraged!

Such things as enrolment forms, and correspondence between the Land Girls and their county committees, were never lodged at Balcombe as women were paid by the farmers not by the Ministry of Agriculture. Further WLA material was lost during the 1944 removal to London, and back; and there were yet more losses in the final return to London at the end of the war. Certainly much of the administrative paperwork belonging to the final phase of the WLA, so the story goes, was burned - although on whose authorisation, and when, remains a mystery. Records preserved at the Public Record Office at Kew are selected, of course, by the creating department, and papers not required are destroyed. The minutes of some War Agricultural Committee meetings lodged at the PRO can only be viewed by special permission. Fortunately, archive material of one kind or another has found its way into libraries and museums, and it was here, after an invaluable 'first dip' into the Public Record Office, that much of the information eventually surfaced.

The women themselves, fortunately, not only hoarded souvenirs of their years on the land, but many had kept wartime diaries, as well as copies of *The Landswomen* and *The Land Girl*. Most important of all were their memories. With few exceptions, the women to whom I have spoken, or who have written to me, recalled their experiences in the Women's Land Army with generosity and enthusiasm, although, naturally, stories of bulls being mistaken for cows are legion! One woman wrote saying she had just seen a television programme that mentioned the Land Army, and only wished that the man who had written it had telephoned her first - then she might have set him straight on a few points. She passed them on to me instead! Another wrote, 'They did not actually say that we were only useful for twenty-one out of every twenty-eight days, but that is what a lot of them meant. What a cheek!'

To all of these, and to the many readers of *Home and Country*, *Farmers Weekly*, *The Townswoman*, and *The Landworker*, who sent in their reminiscences of Land Army days, I offer my sincere thanks.

Carol Twinch

Bawburgh, Norfolk
July 1990

Acknowledgements

The author would like to express her gratitude to those who have assisted her during the writing of this book, in particular:

David Beasley, Librarian, Goldsmiths' Hall; Charles Burrell; Mrs. G. Calthorpe and Mrs. M. Conu, from the Women's Farm and Garden Association; Lord Denman; Professor D.R. Denman; Mrs. Helena Dightam, Information & Research Assistant, The Associated Country Women of the World; Moira Eagling, Editor of *The Townswoman*; Dr. Ruth Gasson; Mrs. P. Greenwood; Penny Kitchen, Editor of *Home & Country*; Mr. Julian Lloyd, Sandringham Estate Office; Mrs. E.M. Lucas, Librarian, Wye College; Mrs. Sheila McIntyre; Mrs. Elsa Morrow; Nigel Nicolson; Mrs. Jean Procter; Lord Selborne; Mr. C.R.G. Shewell-Cooper; Janet E. Smith, Branch Librarian, Wymondham; Baroness Trumpington; Dr. Sadie Ward and Mrs. Barbara Holden of the Institute of Agricultural History, Reading University.

I should like to thank Mr. Tony Cooper of Adprint Ltd. (ECN Special Publications) for permission to use extracts from 'After the Vote'; Eleanor Harland, Forestry Commission Librarian for permission to use extracts from 'Beating About the Bush'; Nigel Nicolson for use of material relating to Vita Sackville-West; and Demelza Spargo for permission to quote from 'This Land is Our Land'. For permission to quote from other published material I should like to thank the following: the British Food & Farming Year Office; Jonathan Cape Ltd. for extracts from *The People's War by Angus Calder*; Chatto & Windus Ltd. for extracts from *Lady Denman GBE* by Gervas Huxley; W.H. Heinemann Ltd. for extracts from *Organization Woman* by Mary Stott; National Federation of Women's Institutes for quotations from *Women's Institutes* by Cicely McCall, *Jam and Jerusalem* by Simon Goodenough, and *The History of the Women's Institute Movement of England and Wales* by Inez Jenkins; Pan Books for quotation from *Love, Sex and War* by John Costello; Times Newspapers Ltd. for extracts from *The Times*; and the Young Women's Christian Association of Great Britain for use of extracts from 'Our Outlook'.

My thanks are also due to Anglia Television Ltd.; The Edinburgh School of Agriculture; Harper Adams Agricultural College; the Ministry of Agriculture, Fisheries & Food Library; Newnham College Library, Cambridge; and the Royal Agricultural Society of England.

1

Do Your Bit!

During my three recent visits to France I have been so much impressed by the amount of work done by old men, women and children. The women seem none the worse for it, and I believe it would be a splendid thing if we could get the women on the land in this country too.

M. P. A. Hankey, Secretary to the War Cabinet, in July, 1915

For almost a century, following the ending of the wars against Napoleon, Britain, with a few alarms and excursions, had contrived to avoid either revolution or involvement in a major conflict on the mainland of Europe. With the peace had come the expansion of trade and of Empire. The Royal Navy dominated the oceans and provided protection for the huge British merchant fleet which supplied the needs of what, even in 1914, was still the world's foremost industrial nation. Imperial might, however, tended to mask less acceptable realities; not merely the huge gulf that separated rich and poor, but the contrast between industrial enterprise and agricultural depression.

Although domestic agriculture had shown some recovery from the trough of the 1880s, years of under-investment had left the rural economy in a desperate state, with farms neglected, profits eroded, and farm workers disadvantaged. If life for some of the larger landowners jogged along pleasantly enough, the families of most smallholders and agricultural workers were less fortunate.

The opening up of the North American prairies, and the shift from sail to steam; improvements in railways overseas, some - like those in Argentina - largely funded by British investment; the introduction of refrigeration: all made possible the swift transportation of essential foodstuffs to the ports, from which they could be shipped at prices undercutting those of domestic British producers. In this way, huge quantities of grain were imported from North America, mutton from Australia, mutton and lamb from New Zealand, and beef from the Argentine. In April 1913 the *Farmer and Stock-Breeder* reported increased imports of bacon, eggs, barley, oats, maize, and potatoes - over two million hundredweight of which had been imported from Germany. While perishable foodstuffs, such as milk, fruit, and vegetables, still provided the home producer with a reasonable return, there was a twenty-five per cent reduction in the total acreage of corn grown in Britain between 1896 and the First World War. By 1914 she imported fifty per cent of the food required to feed a population of some thirty-six million people, three-quarters of whom lived in towns.

When war was declared in 1914, the Royal Navy, as in the previous century, was able to impose an increasingly effective blockade of the enemy coast. Nor, in the event, was the German High Seas fleet able to mount an effective challenge to British naval supremacy. However, the German Government *was* in a position to organise a counter-blockade of the British Isles by use of submarines, or U-Boats, in what, for Allied shipping, was to prove one of the costliest campaigns of the war. In the pre-war years, German strategists had noted Britain's increasing dependence on imported food, and were confident that a submarine blockade would starve her into submission. Indeed, there were many in Britain itself who believed that the German intelligence network was better-informed as to the true state of British agriculture than was the British Government.

The Prime Minister, H. H. Asquith, supported by the President of the Board of Trade, Walter Runciman, maintained his faith in the Report of the Royal Commission on Agriculture (1903), which had stated that the country's dependence upon imported food was not significant, and that there was little risk of a total cessation of supplies. The Commission had seen no reason for government measures to protect domestic agriculture, then, or in the immediate future; consequently, in September 1914, the Government informed the House of Commons that it did not feel justified in giving farmers financial inducements to increase cereal acreage.

One man who well-understood the implications of an over-reliance on high levels of imported food was William Waldegrave Palmer, the second Earl of Selborne, who, as First Lord of the Admiralty in 1900, had presided over the introduction of submarines into the Royal Navy. Appointed President of the Board of Agriculture in May 1915, he knew that the administration he joined had little idea how serious any interruption of imported foodstuffs was likely to be in the event of prolonged hostilities. While Lord Selborne argued, with perfect logic, that at the time the Royal Commission had reported, in 1903, Britain was not at war, he had to contend with the arguments of Walter Runciman (himself President of the Board of Agriculture between 1911-14), who used his authority to convince the Cabinet that civilian food supplies would be maintained without the necessity of State involvement. He also persuaded them that there was no need to regulate prices, nor to heed calls for a Ministry of Food. Although Lord Selborne urged his colleagues to consider the problems of home food production as a matter of urgency, his pleas were disregarded. Not until December 1916 was a Ministry of Food established, and it was to be

December 1917, with the U-Boat blockade at its height, and the country only three weeks from starvation, before food rationing was finally introduced.

Lacking support from his Cabinet colleagues, Lord Selborne, nevertheless, started to do what he could by way of propaganda. He accepted that any appeal for increased food production would initially have to be made on patriotic rather than pecuniary grounds. Farmers had to be persuaded to grow the crops that would keep Britain fed, despite a reduced labour force - over-zealous recruitment by the Army having removed many skilled men from the farms - and some hasty changes in agricultural policy. Before 1914, any increase in the cost of wartime food would merely have forced stricter economies at home, whilst the incentive of monetary reward would have spurred output.

On the 16 July 1915, Mr Asquith answered Lord Selborne's personal plea for the food situation to be taken seriously. There was not, in his opinion, 'the least fear that any probable or conceivable development of German submarine activity can be a serious menace to our food supply.'

If, by 1915, the Cabinet was aware of the potential seriousness of the situation there was no wholesale change in attitude. Lord Selborne commissioned a series of reports to look at the problem, but they only tentatively suggested that things were 'poor' in rural Britain. On the 17 June 1915, he set up a Committee to look into the ways in which home food production might be organised. Under the chairmanship of Viscount Milner, Selborne's friend and mentor, the Committee included Row-land Prothero (later Lord Ernle), who was to succeed Lord Selborne as President of the Board of Agriculture in December 1916, and the Rt. Hon. Francis Acland.

In its first report, the Milner Committee advocated a national agricultural policy, and proposed a series of official and unofficial debates on the problems of food scarcity. It also took the opportunity to reinforce the message that shortages inevitably meant greater reliance on home production. It made clear that farmers were expected to change their methods, and to face the certain fact that, in spite of enforced increases in production, prices would inevitably fall when the war ended. It also noted that food distribution needed investigation, a suggestion largely ignored until December 1916.

Some of the Milner recommendations were implemented in the autumn of 1915, but only after Lord Selborne's tireless, if gentlemanly, harassment of the Prime Minister. A secret Enclosure, printed only for the use of the Cabinet, emphasised a new awareness:

> We cannot make war without taking risks, but there are some risks which we have no right to take if we can make any provision against them. One of those risks is invasion, and another is shortage of the food of the people. The war may possibly come to an end before the harvest of 1916, but I am afraid that it will not be so. Certainly we cannot be sure that the war will be over by that date, and therefore we must consider the conditions under which we may be waging war subsequent to 1916.

Owing to government inertia, and with Parliament on the eve of adjournment, no more of the Milner recommendations were adopted. However, some progress was made. Before Lord Selborne's resignation, in June 1916, he established, in consultation with Lloyd George, a Food Production Department. This was to constitute a new branch of the Board of Agriculture. A Standing Committee was to be formed within the Department, which met every three or four days between May 1917 and early 1919, to discuss agricultural topics. Lord Selborne also set up a network of War Agricultural Committees (WACs) which were intended to co-ordinate matters relating to agriculture at a local level. These were to prove largely ineffective until the change of administration, in December 1916, when they received the backing of the new Prime Minister, David Lloyd George.

The Food Production Department operated as seven divisions:

Local organisation	Supplies
Technical division	Horticulture (including allotments)
Labour	Women
Cultivation	

A team from the research and agricultural institutes, headed by the Rt. Hon. Francis Acland, was formed to deal with scientific questions. A special Women's Branch, with Miss Meriel Talbot as Director and Mrs Alfred Lyttleton as Deputy, was also formed. Meriel Talbot reported directly to Lord Selborne on the activities of the many recruiting groups as well as co-ordinating the work of the National Union of Women Workers, using the WACs as agents in each county. The Branch was to be officered and staffed entirely by women. Although Miss Talbot expressed a wish that the entire organisation should come under the Board of Agriculture, she agreed to liaise with the Board of Trade as and when necessary.

Few of Britain's farmers had, however, the slightest idea of the national food picture. If pressed, they could furnish a mental tally of personal production in terms of gallons or hundredweight, but it was not their business to assess national stocks. How could they know what the effects of German U-Boat attacks on British shipping might be when the Cabinet itself hardly knew? Over the next two bad harvests, and with government information about wheat shortages, they were able to assess the demands that would be made upon them: traditional pasture would have to be ploughed up to make way for cereals, potatoes, and root crops. They knew, too, that no war lasts for ever, and that sooner or later the bottom would fall out of the inflationary war market and imports be resumed at their former high levels. Quite rightly, no farmer was about to make the mistake of trusting a politician's promise of a bright, more secure, future. In 1914, like most of the population, farmers had assumed that the war would not last long, and that in any event farm workers would be required to stay where they would be of most use. They were therefore unprepared, and angry, when their skilled men were recruited for war service, and indignant (to say the least!) when told that the Government proposed to

4

increase the number of women volunteers being sent on to the land, and that women were to be virtually the only new source of labour.

Some small part of this new workforce was to include women who had been active in the movement for Women's Suffrage, the more militant faction of which (led by Christabel Pankhurst) had, by its violent methods, alienated public sympathy for the movement's aims. Indeed, for the moderate leadership, the war could not have come at a more opportune time. Mrs Pankhurst was confident that the Government, although out of sympathy with the women's demands, would have to acknowledge any co-operation received from that source. In fact, the Government, required to raise two and a half million men for the army, 329,000 men for the navy, and some 60,000 men for the new air force, needed all the support it could muster from those who would help fill the jobs of the absent men. Six days after the declaration of war, all suffragette prisoners were released unconditionally. As the *Daily Herald* reported, on 11 August 1914:

The remission of sentences on the suffrage prisoners was a natural step; for people who have not been slow, at the very onset of this war, to turn to the women for aid.

In addition to the general call, the Board of Agriculture, and the Board of Trade, jointly issued an appeal to women to 'come forward and do your bit' to assist in food production. Women everywhere answered the appeal, many doubtless echoing the words of Mrs Pankhurst herself: 'What is the use of fighting for a vote if we have not got a country to vote in?'

In March 1915, the Government announced that it was compiling a register of women willing to do industrial, agricultural, or clerical work; but confusion existed as to who should be responsible for allocating women to particular jobs. Never a man to miss an opportunity, David Lloyd George, the Minister of Munitions, summoned Mrs Pankhurst to his office in July. Both saw a mutual advantage in appealing to women's patriotism. It was agreed that a demonstration be organised along the lines of those familiar to the Suffragettes but this time with the Government's approval. This would play down the Government's urgent need for labour, and instead demand every woman's 'Right to Serve'. As nothing stimulates indignation so much as the denial of liberty, some thirty thousand women, believing their 'rights' were threatened, attended the 'Call to Women' demonstration! Expenses for the July march were met out of the Propaganda Fund.

Lloyd George was aware of the situation at the Board of Agriculture, and of Mr Hankey's assessment of the role of women in France. He realised that women would prove to be indispensible on the farms, and had decided that an increase in female labour might also assist his own political ambitions. At the end of March he had been rewarded with one million women joining the paid labour force. All manner of jobs now presented themselves to the raw recruits of the labour market, including the offer from an all-male Government (boosting the promise of female emancipation) to step back in time to the muck and mire of near-primitive agriculture. 'Our soldiers must have Food', ran the Government plea, following with the challenge:

> In the past you have asked for opportunities. In the present you have shown what you can do when you are trusted with national work. In the future it must be proved that you can respond to even greater calls.

Women had asked to play a part in society, and now the Government was entrusting them with national work. Although it was to the munitions factories that women volunteers flocked first, such work by no means attracted everyone. Many women already had experience of factory work in the industrial towns, but how many from the towns had experience of the country, or indeed the confidence, to drive a team of horses, wield a pitchfork, or feed the noisy, dusty, threshing machines, hungry for stooks of wheat? Farm men said that 'educated' or 'refined' women would never stick at it; neither was the Government entirely convinced. It was for the women themselves to set out to prove the doubters wrong. With such a willing workforce at their disposal it should have been an easy matter for the WACs to utilise the volunteers registered with them. In fact the opposite occurred. Women were to be kept waiting for jobs, while farmers remained suspicious, and rivalries between the several labour agencies simply compounded the chaos. Indeed, it was in spite, rather than because of, the legion of committees and sub-committees, and the wrangling between government Boards, that women got on to the land at all.

Food has to be grown, and this involves time, much hard work, and is always carried out at the mercy of the weather. It was one thing to persuade women to enter munitions factories by presenting an idyllic image of a rural Britain, with its ancient churches and thatched cottages, requiring protection from the ravening Hun; it was much more difficult to convey the *realities* of agriculture in anything like so attractive a way. It required a specific campaign. Consequently, both the Board of Agriculture and the Board of Trade issued an appeal to women's consciences - stating that nowhere near enough women had come forward, although there had in reality been a remarkable response. The problem was that the WACs were impossibly slow in processing the women who were enlisting. While recruits were registered for agricultural work, the administrators were unable to get them to the areas where they were most needed. Emergencies demand immediate solutions: a crop ready for harvest may be soaked in a matter of hours, and cows needing to be milked have a limited waiting capacity. It often happened that by the time the Local Register had been consulted, and a suitable woman found, it was too late for her to be of any practical use. As Viscountess Wolseley observed in her book *Women and the Land*, (1916):

> In vain each day we scan the papers, hoping to find that the register of voluntary and paid women workers, made many months ago, will at length be more vigorously utilised.

Shortly after the War Agricultural Committees had been set up, Lord Selborne directed that they should devote some time to the training of women for farm work. Unfortunately, this suggestion foundered almost immediately. Placing women where they were most needed was only part of a wider responsibility - that of implementing changes in farming practices. To require War Agricultural Committees to organise such training was asking too much of them. The lack of resources, and the clumsy bureaucracy meant that only piecemeal training was given, or offered, to the 40,000 women whose names were on one or other of the WAC Registers.

As early as the autumn of 1915, Lord Selborne had seen the need for special committees to deal with women's farm labour. Special Women's WACs were formed, and, in November that year, he issued a circular to the new WWACs again relating to the specific training of women in agriculture. He urged them to try and work with, rather than in opposition to, the Labour Exchanges or any other local committees they came across. Women available for work were henceforth to be divided into two classes:

(i) those women resident in the villages,

(ii) those women brought in from outside, and requiring training.

This may have been a somewhat broad division, but it represented a beginning. Lord Selborne also wished to take advantage of the activities, and advice, of several reputable agencies like the Women's Farm Land Union, and the Agricultural Section of the Women's Legion. Central organisation remained elusive, however, until the Women's Branch of the Food Production Department began issuing weekly labour charts for each county. These attempted to show every district in which a demand for labour existed. The Women's Branch had its own Labour Committee, representing members of the Ministry of Labour and Ministry of National Service, the Women's National Land Service Corps (WNLSC), the University Association of Land Workers, and the Flax Production Branch of the Board of Agriculture. The Labour Committee was also intended to help meet seasonal and emergency labour requirements. Flax, for example, was grown at the request of the War Office and the Air Ministry, and often required emergency helpers. Although flax production was to prove unsuccessful in terms of final yield it entailed much labour, a large proportion being women.

The WNLSC had been founded in 1914, at the behest of Lord Milner, and was one of the largest groups to have a representative on the Labour Committee. In 1916 it claimed to have placed 870 women on the land, and 'knew of many more'. Its Chairman was Mrs Roland Wilkins. Lord Selborne was able to secure a grant for the WNLSC, proportionate to such sums as were raised voluntarily. The women of the WNLSC usually had some farm training, and they were later to act as foremen and instructors for the unskilled recruits of the Women's Land Army. Much of the organisation of the WNLSC was carried out by members of the Women's Farm and Garden Union (WGFU) which had been formed in 1910. This was to prove invaluable in the cause of education and training, and in 1916 was credited with training 627 women, many of whom were, in turn, to help organise the untrained Women's Land Army.

'Doing one's bit' remained the clarion call. Indeed, for the first two years of the war, volunteering was very nearly a national vocation for both men and women. Alone among the belligerents, Britain had relied wholly upon volunteers to man its forces. By May 1916, and in the light of the quite appalling losses on the Western Front, Parliament realised that volunteers were not enough, and passed the General Compulsion Bill, which made military service obligatory for all males between eighteen and forty-one years of age. Trades Unions were no longer able to argue that women were undermining the employment of male workers, but as far as agriculture was concerned, Lord Selborne was aware that the momentum of persuasion and enrolment had still to be maintained. The question was *how*?

Demonstrations

One answer came from Cornwall. According to W. H. Walter, Honorary Secretary of the Launceston District War Agricultural Committee, Cornish women were nettled by the farm workers' attitude that they were not good enough to take a man's place on the land. After a series of heated letters to local newspapers, a novel demonstration of women's work on the land was staged at Launceston on 9 March 1916. The demonstration caught on. The Launceston example was shortly to be followed by one in Truro, held on 7 April. The Chairman of the Cornwall WAC, Alderman Hawk, said of the Truro event:

> The work was most creditable and astonished a number of farmers. If any criticisms were to be passed, it would be with respect to the arrangements of some of the stewards. The women, the majority of whom claim to be but learners, were required to do what could not be expected even of skilled labourers. In the ploughing class, for example, they had to start with new ploughs, stiff with paint, to open up a straight furrow through a long field, with only a single mark to aim at.

His comments regarding the behaviour of the stewards, also extended to the problems of harnessing the draught horses:

> Harnessing horses was another branch of work where the women might have received a little more consideration. Several of the horses were between 16 and 17 hands high, and it was unreasonable to expect women of medium height to lift the heavier part of the harness clean on the horse's back ... many short expert horsemen had always found it necessary to get on to a step or block of some kind to harness all horses; no such provision was made for the women. Even the most cautious critic, however, could not fail to admit that the women handled the horses splendidly.

The second Earl of Selborne (1859-1942),
who was President of the Board of Agriculture from May 1915 until June 1916.

There was further praise for the women. One of the organisers said that although potato planting had often been described as a woman's job, it had always been understood that this was merely placing the sets in the rows. Now, however, 'these women not only placed the sets, but, with spade and fork, formed the necessary straight rows, and completed the work of tilling in admirable fashion.'

After the outstanding success of these, and similar, demonstrations the Board of Agriculture acted with commendable speed. A circular letter sent out to all the Women's War Agricultural Committees, in May 1916, by Sidney Olivier, the Permanent Secretary, informed them that Lord Selborne had been very pleased with reports of the demonstrations, and that all counties should use this method of showing farmers that women were capable of performing satisfactorily the many forms of farm work. It added the President's hope that the committees would become better organised, so that there might be simultane-

9

ous demonstrations throughout the nation during the week beginning 5 June. This, as it turned out, would be Lord Selborne's last month as President before he handed over his responsibilities to the Earl of Crawford & Balcarres.

While some of the WACs were extremely tardy, many did try their best to organise public displays of women's work. Representatives of the Board of Trade, and the Board of Agriculture were often on hand at such demonstrations to talk to farmers, and to persuade some of them to take on women there and then. In June, Sidney Olivier himself was present at the Manchester venue of the Royal Agricultural Society of England's Show, to witness the Women Workers' Demonstration: the object of which was to emphasise the vital necessity of producing home-grown food, and to show that women could 'take a useful part in the work of the farms, and by their patriotism and self-sacrifice save the situation'. Four acres of land had been allocated for demonstrations of ploughing, working and preparing the land for a turnip crop, and milking and tending cattle. Twelve women took part, and the whole thing was arranged by the Lancashire and Cheshire County Committees for Employment of Women. Miss La Mothe, who had been a member of the Women's Mission to French Farms, was on hand to represent the Board of Trade. The demonstrations were held from 10 a.m. until midday, and from 2 p.m. until 5 p.m. on all three days. Any farmers requiring women land workers were required to obtain full particulars at the Labour Exchange stand on the Showground - and therein lay one of the biggest obstacles to supplying farmers with the labour they needed.

While other industries or occupations might be adequately supplied, little expertise being needed on the part of the Labour Exchange Officer, agriculture necessitated dealing with individual farmers - men used to running their business in their own way, and with particular seasonal labour problems which were not always understood by Board of Trade clerks. The Labour Exchange Act (1909) had made all employment the responsibility of the Board of Trade, although the Board of Agriculture was in a better position to assess and to provide for the needs of the farming community. Disagreement between the Presidents of the two Boards over the employment of agricultural labour did nothing to improve the situation. Nor were the differences simply over labour jurisdiction. The Board of Trade had powers to requisition food stocks if, in its opinion, they were being unreasonably withheld. Although never used, Board of Trade officials spent much valuable time compiling seemingly endless lists of retail prices, and they were to clash continually with Board of Agriculture officials. Co-operation between the officers of both Boards degenerated to such an extent that the Government was forced to resolve the matter by transferring the entire responsibility for women's farm labour to the Board of Agriculture. The Board of Trade was to co-operate where necessary, but was relieved of any responsibility for training or negotiations about wages. It was at this stage almost impossible to know exactly how many women were working, how many were part-time, or how many had had any form of training, as Board of Trade figures are extremely unclear. However, a summary of War Agricultural

Committee returns to the Board of Agriculture, for August 1916, reveals that (although not all the Committees had reported back) 57,487 women were registered in thirty counties, but only 28,767 were at work. It was known, of course, that many more women throughout the country were actually working than the figures revealed. In certain counties, like Wiltshire, Devon, and parts of Lincolnshire, as well as in Wales, large numbers of women had traditionally worked on the land, and many of these had never registered regarding it as an 'unnecessary fuss'. A previous return for Lincolnshire had shown that there were 2,041 women at work, while only 599 were on the register.

Gradually, a possible route emerged for the innocently eager volunteers. Those not enlisting with one of the voluntary agencies were initially required to appear before the WACs, which would assess their potential worth by means of an interview. If they passed this stage successfully the village correspondent would be notified, and a job allocated. The Committees were largely made up of representatives of the local County Council, farmers' associations, agricultural colleges, education authorities, local Members of Parliament, and certain 'county ladies'. As the Committees were self-elected, and voluntary, they conformed to no particular standard, and consequently accepted referrals from any source. Some operated autonomously, only answering government circulars where necessary. Although acting as the official recruitment agency for women land workers they had still to compete with other voluntary bodies doing the same thing. Influential women, like Lady Londonderry, started to organise women's land work through the Women's Legion, which started life in December 1914 as the Women's Reserve, and had attracted some initial hostility, owing to a general disapproval of trained and disciplined women in uniform. In the Legion's case, and after lengthy discussions with Lord Selborne, it was given a government grant of several hundred pounds, and administered its own Agricultural Section. It is probable that some women were better-persuaded by such organisations than by the WACs. Certainly, many siezed the opportunity of setting up private employment agencies, and their methods of operation occasioned the issuing of a statement in July 1916:

> The Board of Agriculture . . . understands that fees are being asked for by certain agencies as a condition of offering to find employment for women on the land. The Board wish it to be clearly understood that payments are unnecessary in view of the arrangements made in their authority for this purpose, particulars of which can be obtained on application to the Secretary of the Board.

The other major stumbling block to the easy acceptance of women as farmworkers concerned the matter of wages. Mrs Pankhurst's 'Call to Women' may have produced a willing army, but farmworkers, like their male counterparts in the cities, did not take kindly to the influx of women. Trades Unions in general were unsympathetic to the concept of women at work, and nowhere more than on the farms. The position of the male farmworker prior to the war had been precarious; now there were fewer jobs available, and these carried with them no formal minimum wage. At first the prospect of war had not caused them undue alarm, rather the contrary. After the initial plundering of the farms by the War Office recruiting machine, farmwork was recognised as being of prime importance to the nation. Understandably, farmworkers begrudged the recruitment of un-skilled female labour, particularly as this would mean releasing men to the fighting services. There was also the feeling that his scarcity value should be reflected in higher wages; if untrained women received virtually the same wages as he did, it would be more than merely adding insult to injury. Farmworkers felt undermined, disadvantaged, and rather insulted.

The Government attempted to resolve this crisis by setting up a Wages Board, as part of the Corn Production Act passed early in 1917. Its first Chairman was Sir Ailwyn Fellowes, a past President of the Board of Agricul-ture. The Wages Board was to investigate farm wages, fixing them from time to time, and to review the wages needed by a labourer to keep 'himself and his family in such a state of health as would enable him to be an efficient labourer'.

Lord Selborne saw the wages question as being linked to the price the farmer could expect for his wheat; if the return could be guaranteed at a minimum of 45s. a quarter, the suggested statutory wage was affordable. It was his opinion that,

> the effect of the guarantee will be permanent, and the land which has been ploughed up will remain under the plough, and the rate of wages of agriculture will remain raised after the guarantee has come to an end, even should the price of wheat fall once again to what it was before the war, which I do not myself expect.

The National Union of Agricultural Workers, which had been re-formed in 1907, greeted the 1917 Wages Board with reserved enthusiasm. The dilemma for the Union was its commitment to a fair deal for *all* farm workers. The General Secretary of the Union, George Edwards, was to make the position clear in a letter addressed to British women, from his Fakenham home, on 3 January 1916:

> The crisis is so great . . . that I venture to make this appeal to you to offer your services in cultivating the land in order that as much food can be produced at home as possible. There will be a great deal of work to do in the spring, such as hoeing and weeding, getting the land fit for the turnip crops, and many light jobs which hitherto have been done by men; and as there is a great shortage of labour we will see that fair wages shall be offered to you. One of the first essentials of life is food, and if this cannot be produced then a great disaster is staring us in the face. To prevent this our womankind are called to help. I therefore appeal to you in the name of God, who made you free, and in the interests of your children to help in this hour of need.

Riddling potatoes, c. 1915-16.
Land Army girls working on Mr J. Thisleton-Smith's farm at West Barsham, Norfolk.

In January 1917, for the first time, workers on the land were guaranteeed a new minimum wage fixed at 25s. a week. At the same time, the Army Council agreed to treat women as supplementary to, rather than as a substitute for, farm men. The fear remained, however, that if women were employed permanently on farms, the men would become liable for military service. There had also been a suspicion that District Registrars, who were the Board of Trade's officers, might place a woman on a farm and then pass on the name of any man there to the Tribunals and Military Representatives. The Board of Agriculture had reassured the Union that this was unlikely, but it was one more reason for men to mistrust the allocation of women labourers.

Happily, not even the Military Representatives could envisage a Britain totally bereft of its farm men; nor could the countrywomen, whose own welcome to the new female workforce tended to be cool. The working farmer's wife no doubt saw only another mouth to feed; but labourers' wives could see the prospect of their men being ousted from their jobs and made liable for military service, and village women thought that their casual or part-time jobs might be affected.

Lady Denman

Much of the pioneering work to improve the position of women was performed by a class of educated women brought up in the Victorian tradition of philanthropy, who were able, by virtue of their wealth or their husband's position, to put their influence in the community to good use. There can be few better examples of this indomitable, pioneering, tradition than Lady Denman. Born in November 1884, Gertrude Mary Pearson was the only daughter of W. D. Pearson, afterwards first Viscount Cowdray. She married Lord Thomas Denman in 1903, and when news of the murder of the Archduke Franz Ferdinand at Sarejevo reached them, the couple were already on their way home from Australia, where Lord Denman had been Governor General. Once on dry land, Lady Denman had wasted no time in master-minding the charity 'Smokes for Wounded Soldiers and Sailors Society' (SSS), and had , together with her friend Nellie Grant, started a backyard poultry-keeping information service. Towards the end of 1916, after Mrs Grant had rejoined her husband in Spain, Lady Denman began an association with the Women's Institute movement that was to last until her death in 1954. In October 1916 she was offered, and accepted, the position of Chairman of the Women's Institute sub-committee of the Agricultural Organisation Society (AOS). The Institutes had been started in Canada in 1897 by Adelaide Hunter Hoodless, after her baby died as a result of drinking contaminated milk. The idea of the Institutes was brought to Britain by a fellow-Canadian, Mrs Alfred Watt, who, following the death of her husband, decided to live in England, and discerned on her arrival the need for a similar organisation for countrywomen. Drawing upon her experience as Secretary of the Advisory Board of Women in the Department of Agriculture, British Columbia, she spoke at a meeting of the Agricultural Organisation Society, which was formed in 1901 to help local farming co-operatives. The AOS, on the advice of Mr Nugent Harris, backed the idea of the Institutes and acted as guardian to the infant movement. In fact the movement had grown so fast that by October, 1916, it needed a Chairman, and it was this responsibility that Lady Denman took on. A year later she was to become Chairman of the National Federation of Women's Institutes (NFWI).

When, by the autumn of 1917, it became clear that the Institutes had outgrown the resources of the AOS, it was proposed that instead they should operate as a special section of the Women's Branch of the Food Production Department: a move welcomed by Rowland Prothero, who had set up the Women's Branch at the beginning of the year, shortly after his appointment as President of the Board of Agriculture.

With the NFWI under the wing of the Women's Branch it was indeed fortunate that Lady Denman and Meriel Talbot, the Director of the Women's Branch, saw eye to eye on most matters. Lady Denman had been worried that the move to incorporate the Institutes into a Government body might prejudice the movement's independence, by surrendering its liberty to lay down its own policies and functions.

The AOS continued to give advice and assistance in setting up the Institutes, usually with the help of existing local garden or allotment societies; Lady Denman did not entirely approve of the male dominance of the Society, feeling that too few women were involved in discussions on local farm co-operatives, and that in general they were not taken seriously. After some discussion, Lady Denman further agreed to act for the Women's Branch as Honorary Assistant Director to Meriel Talbot, with Mrs Watt as organiser. The relationship between Mrs Watt, described as 'a small assertive woman . . . with magnetic dark eyes', and Lady Denman was not always so harmonious. As Simon Goodenough remarked in *Jam and Jerusalem*:

> According to Mrs Dorothy Drage, who knew her well, Mrs Watt was 'already at the top of the mountain', while 'everyone else was at the foothills'. Without her, there is no doubt that the WI would have taken a lot longer to reach England. Lady Denman would never have started the WI, though she ran it superbly. It was the clash between these two personalities - the idealist and the organiser - that caused some of the early creative tension of the WI.

Disastrous harvests, the German U-Boat attacks on British shipping, and outbreaks of civil unrest caused by the ensuing food shortages, were to bring matters to a climax. By the summer, Rowland Prothero conceded that unless there was better co-ordination of farm labour there would be no harvest at all in 1918. Production not only had to be maintained, it needed to be increased. In addition, some two million more acres would have to be brought into cultivation to meet the targets set for the 1918 harvest. Within the Women's Branch, plans were drawn up to organise a mobile force of women farm workers, the Women's Land Army. Rowland Prothero, who had been a member of the Milner Committee, announced that the formation of the WLA was linked with the Government's stated desire to regenerate country life, and to assist with the extension of smallholdings and allotments. With only three weeks' supply of food remaining in the country there were, possibly, more pressing reasons!

The Women's Land Army

The Women's Land Army, funded by the Government, and under the direction of Meriel Talbot, was designed to be a force ready to go where and when it was most needed. As Assistant Director, Lady Denman was directly involved in all Women's Branch activities, but nowhere more so than in the establishment of, and recruitment for, the WLA.

In the early years of the war, demonstrations at the County shows had been used not simply to recruit women, but also to persuade farmers to *use* women workers. By 1917, however, many of these shows had ceased to function, and demonstrations like that held at the Manchester 'Royal' had a very limited audience, and one already involved in farming. Held in populated areas, such shows were no more likely to reach would-be WLA recruits from the rural areas than government propaganda or recruiting publicity. It was decided therefore, that open-air rallies would be more appropriate. So Lady Denman and Nellie Grant (once more returned from Spain), dressed in Land Army uniform, drove around the Southern Counties in a small car holding open-air meetings. Gervas Huxley, in his biography of Lady Denman, describes a typical rally:

> Stopping the car in the middle of the High Street or in the Market Place of the towns, one of them would attract the public's startled attention by rotating a policeman's very heavy wooden alarm rattle, which made an ear-splitting noise. After this, the other would make a rousing speech standing on the top of the car. Sometimes they were invited to use the stage of theatres or cinemas, and once, in Portsmouth, they followed a turn by performing dogs, and had a riotous reception from a sailor audience.

Sometimes the duo would join in a similar parade with the WRNS or the WAACs. On one occasion they found that a seven mile march through Southampton was planned, so 'they hired horses from a livery stable and formed the only mounted element in the procession, refuting the protests of the organisers by insisting that horses were indubitably agricultural.'! During their travels they would often take advantage of hospitality offered by friends in the large households of country estates, and were only too apt to discover that they had just signed on a friend's last remaining housemaid!

The Women's Branch at first managed the training of women for service in the Woods and Forests Department of the Board of Agriculture. A Women's Forestry Service (WFS) was also formed in 1917, and at its peak this totalled some 2,000 members, roughly divided between timber measuring and general forest work. The Women's Forestry Service was later extended to include women required by the Timber Supply Department of the Board of Trade. In September 1917, the Women's Branch took on responsibility for supplying women labour for the all-important Forage Committee of the War Office. Both the Women's Forestry Service and the Forage Section, however, were withdrawn from the authority of the Women's Branch, and by the time this was stood down, in 1919, only the Women's Land Army remained operative.

Women joining the agricultural workforce had also to face the often daunting task of enrolment - a procedure that might well have been made easier; although in truth it ought to have prepared them for the rigours to come! However, as tensions between the Board of Agriculture and the Board of Trade eased, and as the war situation became so critical that it could no longer be ignored, farmers reluctantly accustomed themselves to the use of female farm labour. Rowland Prothero (Lord Ernle), writing in *English Farming Past and Present* estimated that the Women's Branch provided 300,000 part-time

W.L.A.2

WOMEN'S LAND ARMY.

CONDITIONS AND TERMS.

There are three Sections of the Women's Land Army:

    (1). **AGRICULTURE.**

    (2). **TIMBER CUTTING.**

    (3). **FORAGE.**

If you sign on for A YEAR and are prepared to go wherever you are sent, you can join which Section you like.

YOU PROMISE—

1. To sign on in the Land Army for ONE YEAR.
2. To come to a Selection Board when summoned.
3. To be medically examined, free of cost.
4. To be prepared if PASSED by the Selection Board to take up work after due notice.
5. TO BE WILLING TO GO TO WHATEVER PART OF THE COUNTRY YOU ARE SENT.

THE GOVERNMENT PROMISES—

1. AN INITIAL WAGE to workers of 20/- a week. After they have passed an efficiency test the wages given are 22/- a week and upwards.
2. A short course of FREE INSTRUCTION if necessary.
3. FREE UNIFORM.
4. FREE MAINTENANCE in a Depot for a term not exceeding 4 weeks if the worker is OUT OF EMPLOYMENT through no fault of her own.
5. FREE RAILWAY travelling, when taking up or changing Employment.

——————— OR, ———————

If you sign on for only six months, you can join the Agricultural and Timber Cutting Sections, but not the Forage.

YOU PROMISE—

1. To sign on in the Land Army for 6 MONTHS.
2. To come to a Selection Board when summoned.
3. To be medically examined, free of cost.
4. To be prepared if PASSED by the Selection Board to take up work after due notice.
5. TO BE WILLING TO GO TO ANY PART OF THE COUNTRY YOU ARE SENT.

THE GOVERNMENT PROMISES—

1. AN INITIAL WAGE of 20/- per week.
2. UNIFORM FREE.
3. FREE MAINTENANCE in a Depot for a term not exceeding 2 weeks, if the worker is out of employment through no fault of her own.
4. FREE RAILWAY travelling when taking up or changing employment.

NOTE.—No training is given, therefore the initial wage is only 20/-. Should the worker be able to pass an efficiency test, it will be raised to 22/-. Two weeks' maintenance in a depot only is allowed.

(31397) Wt. 18396.95. 500,000 2/18. P. & S. (R.), Ltd (E2633).

[P.T.O.

Conditions and terms set out for those volunteerng to serve in
the 1917 Women's Land Army.

women workers, and a Land Army that at its peak had a strength of 16,000 members. In July 1918, the Board stated that there were 113,000 women workers helping out on the land, and between May 1917 and May 1919, some 23,000 women were to pass through the training centres set up in the counties. One set of returns, taken in August 1918, and relating to 12,637 women was broken down into occupations to show a fairly average picture:

5,734 milkers	260 ploughmen
3,971 field workers	84 thatchers
635 carters	21 shepherds
293 tractor drivers	

The remaining 1,639 were distributed among miscellaneous branches of farming and horticulture.

Once the Women's Land Army got under way, an applicant could be fairly optimistic that she would be placed on a farm. However, she was to be warned by the President of the Board of Agriculture himself that it was no occasion for 'lilac sun-bonnets', and by the women running the village registers that there might well be periods of inactivity caused by seasonal expansion and contraction of work. Not surprisingly it was during such times that many were lured away by higher wages or better conditions elsewhere. Farm work was back-breaking, the wages low, and the status negligible; nevertheless, many women stayed, and saw the job through. Even countrywomen, some with children, were to join in aspects of farm life that they had barely glimpsed before, as it was often easier for the WACs to recruit local women than to bring in official Land Army members from outside. Some enlightened county organisers even arranged crèche facilities to encourage local women. In Lincolnshire, the Holland Committee in particular regarded nursery facilities as essential, and fostered their establishment throughout the country.

The harvest of 1918 was later to be considered the peak of wartime production. The shortage of artificial fertilizers, and the likelihood of poor yields from newly-turned pasture in an age before pesticides, provide two reasons why the target of ploughing a further two million acres of grassland was never achieved. Nevertheless, grain yields *were* increased: from 4,300,000 tons in 1916, to six million tons in 1918; and between 1913 and 1918 there was an increase of some three million tons of potatoes. It was estimated that no less than 100,000 notices were served on farmers or landowners by the WACs - compelling them to plough all grazing land, and to cultivate it for the harvest of 1919. While the majority complied there were to be two hundred and fifty-four prosecutions for default. In 1918, under the Defence of the Realm regulations, the WACs took possession of badly-farmed land totalling 27,287 acres, and arranged for its cultivation, or farmed it themselves, often using the WLA for labour.

2

Ladies on the Land

Without soldiers and munitions the war can not be ended; without food it cannot be prolonged.

President of the Board of Agriculture, 1915

Those familiar with modern farming may find it hard to grasp just what general farmwork entailed for those women starting out as farm workers in the First World War. The working day comprised nine or ten hours hard work, normally starting well before dawn, for which the labourer received a shilling wage. There were mangolds and turnips to be pulled and topped by hand, loaded by fork, and then carted by horse to be clamped in a frost free 'cave' to serve as winter fodder. Hand milking was a necessity, carried out in the early morning (sometimes after feeding the horses) and again at night, after a long day in the fields. There were cold mornings, frozen fingers, and little reliable light. Mud-caked skirts took hours to dry in often damp, draughty rooms, while hot water might entail a long wait for a very little. Imagine, too, the physical effort needed to lift the harness of a working horse, and then to pace mile after exhausting mile over rough ground for hours behind various implements of cultivation in a variety of weathers. No wonder one Dartmoor farmer was overheard to say, 'No woman could stand it; no matter what Lord Selborne says!'

For recruits, the Women's Land Army (WLA) offered a choice of three sections:

(i) The Agriculture Section
Broadly, this was concerned with two types of crop. One, potatoes, corn, and horticultural produce, went directly to feed humans; the second, fodder, to maintain or fatten animals, providing by-products such as milk, cheese, or eggs. Most farms at that time were mixed, and it was grudgingly presumed that a woman might master the art of milking, or be relied upon to tend the young stock. Lambing was also considered highly suitable work for female recruits.

Farm workers, of necessity, were skilled in a variety of tasks; the question was, were women also capable of similar flexibility? Women, it was felt, were only semi-trainable, and, in consequence, only half-useful.

Root crops proved to be of prime importance, and most women volunteers were involved in growing them at some time in their service. Roots: mangolds, potatoes, fodder beet, and turnips, required a relatively high expenditure of labour. They were an invaluable necessity not only in terms of good husbandry, but because of their calorific value to humans as well as to animals. Growing potatoes became every farmer's duty, although he lacked the sophisticated harvesting machinery of today; manufacturers of agricultural implements and machinery as well as fertilizers were, in any case, employed in making munitions, so that the task of planting and harvesting potatoes by hand made necessary many onerous hours of backbreaking work in the open fields. Mangolds and turnips were pulled by hand and laid in rows or piles, and then they had to be hand-loaded or forked into the carts. Back at the farm there was sorting to be done, and more loading and unloading. Some mechanical aids were available to those with the money to invest, and occasionally a group of farmers would co-purchase an item. Inevitably the system broke down when all the shareholders wanted to use the machine at the same time. It was, in any event, not a system that contributed much to the peace of the countryside. Regrettably, it has to be acknowledged that co-operation is not generally one of the more notable virtues of the British farmer!

Hoeing was an inevitable part of root crop work, and in Wales gangs of women were used. In August 1916, girls from the University College of Wales (UCW) in Aberystwyth, under the guidance of Mr and Mrs Stapledon, formed themselves into a mobile hoeing force. Much of the turnip singling in Cardiganshire had been 'hand and knee' work, and many of the farmers were sceptical about the efficiency of women with hoes, but they were to prove effective. Sometimes, when working with swedes that had been allowed to grow too big, the girls had to work in twos, one 'knocking out' while the other did the final singling, each changing places occasionally to avoid tedium. During hot weather the gang started work at 5.30 a.m., working until 8.00 a.m., and then taking a break until 4.00 p.m. Before 1914, piece-work rates of pay varied between 1½d. to 2d. per 100 yards, but by 1916 the rates had increased to between 3d. and 4½d. per 100 yards, according to the condition of the crop. During July and August the students camped out for ease of mobility.

Women from Aberystwyth continued to assist with land work for the duration of the war. Some, from Alexander Hall, under the direction of Miss C. P. Tremain, the Warden, were particularly involved in land work during the long vacations. A 'gang' of students, one UCW Report noted, 'have been working on the land near Bow Street, and small groups of students, or individual workers have taken part in fruit picking and farm work elsewhere.' Many were already engaged in potato planting, and stone-picking, two of the most notorious backbreakers, while one group even formed a gang of flax-pullers in Somerset.

(ii) The Forage Section

The Forage Corps had been the first real attempt by the Government to organise women volunteers, and it represented a challenge for everyone concerned. While the Army relied at first on volunteer recruits to do the fighting, it was unable to obtain the necessary horse-power other than by requisition. The ensuing depletion in the number of farm horses helped accelerate their decline in agriculture, and affected even more the traditional fabric of village life. As Lord Ernle, in his book *The Land and Its People*, observed:

> In October 1917, in 26 administrative counties, the shops of 515 blacksmiths and 216 wheelwrights were closed, and those of 706 blacksmiths and 428 wheelwrights were understaffed. Some of the farm horses were unshod, others comandeered.

Some 256,000 horses were to be lost by the British Army on the Western Front, by one means or another, and their withdrawal from the farms contributed to the farmers' problems. Women were to have a great deal to do with the provision of fodder for these war horses, both draught and cavalry, and also to play a hitherto unthinkable part in working the horses left behind, which were often old and past their prime, badly shod and difficult to handle.

The WLA inherited a Forage Corps which had, from its formation in 1915, suffered the effects of a dual administration. The work of haymaking, stacking and loading bales, and chaff cutting, had been carried out for the Army under the Forage Department of the War Office. Workers involved in growing hay or oats were subject to the authority of the Women's Army Corps. Officially no special training was required, but when the WLA assumed control in 1917 it instigated special conditions. Women signing on for a minimum six months might join the Agricultural or Timber Cutting Sections, but for the Forage Corps a year's commitment was necessary.

As the work involved the women more closely with the home Army camps, the contract of employment was much stricter, and there were penalties for misbehaviour or slackness. In France, where some women were employed to break in and care for horses and mules, they came under the supervision of the Army Service Corps. Women employed by the Forage Department often had duties above and beyond that of husbandry, as Caroline Dakers records in her book *The Countryside at War*:

> Guarding forage dumps was a frequent occupation of the WLA. Girls stationed at a dump in Ringwood in the New Forest were warned to take plenty of warm underclothes, scarves and blankets to survive the winter nights ... As it was the hay was finally sent to Italy in February 1918 only to be lost at sea when the ship carrying it was torpedoed.

Annie Webb, in Forage Corps uniform, 1917.
Born at Abbotsley, near St. Neots in Huntingdonshire, sixteen year old Annie Webb had been in service in London from the age of eleven, before joining the Forage Corps.

(iii) The Forestry Section

'Our Sailors need wood for their ships' went the Government slogan, 'our soldiers need wood for their railways, their shelters and their aeroplanes. In order to provide timber for the Navy and the army, women must help in the work.'

The familiar chaos in recruitment and administration was nowhere more evident than in the Forestry Corps, established in 1917. One of the Food Department's Travelling Inspectors, Gladys Polt, in a letter written in March 1918, reported that the male representatives of the Timber Department in Oxfordshire were taking girls directly through Labour Exchanges without reference to the Land Army. The girls were not asked to sign any enrolment forms, and although the Labour Exchanges requested that they go through the Selection Committee of the Land Army, the Timber Representative ignored the proposal. The fact that women could apply privately, and with far less fuss, through the Labour Exchanges worried the Selection Committee. The feeling was that unless enrolment worked more smoothly women would be put off applying altogether. It was also likely that women would receive better terms of employment and pay through the Exchanges, thus creating discontent amongst the official WLA girls. As it was, anyone signing on for the minimum six months with the Timber Section might expect to receive 20s. a week, out of which maintenance had to be provided.

Some years later, writing in the Women's Institutes magazine, *Home and Country*, the woman who did most to establish the Forestry Corps, Doris Stapledon, recalled:

> I conceived the idea of employing [the women] in gangs on forestry work in conjunction with educated girls from the National Land Service Corps, and thus started what was later to become the Forestry Corps; I badgered a friend who was the Forestry Commissioner for the area to employ a gang of twenty-five to thirty cutting down a larch plantation, tushing the trees out with horses, and sawing them into logs. The Commissioner thought it a mad scheme, and I confess I felt nervous as to how many legs and feet might get cut to pieces. However, I secured a woodman to teach the girls the art of wielding an axe, and he and I taught the whole gang.

The experiment, due perhaps to an absence of severed limbs, was judged a success, and more gangs and camps were established in Radnorshire and Breconshire. This, though, was only the first step, as Doris Stapledon found out:

> I have vivid recollections of strikes for higher wages, etc., and a whole gang singing songs in the face of a helpless foreman in charge of the work, and his SOS for me to come and settle the strife. However, it was all in a day's work.

Everyday work for members of the Forestry Corps consisted of felling trees and sawing them into lengths, as well as stacking and carting; hard, gruelling labour by any standards. Nor were the women helped by the light tan corduroy breeches they had to wear. These were made from coarse material, and the heavy inside seams chafed uncomfortably. Yet the women who remained were to gain the respect and admiration of their male colleagues.

Registration and Selection

By 1917, any woman responding to the WLA call had first to negotiate the obstacle course of registration. Having decided to sign on, either for six months or a year, the candidate was required to make herself available to appear before a Selection Board when summoned. *Mobility* was the key word: successful applicants were required to go to whatever part of the country the Selection Board thought most appropriate. In return, the Government offered an initial wage of 20s. per week, a free uniform, free maintenace at a Depot for up to two weeks if there was no work, and free rail travel when taking up or changing employment. No training was promised, although the lucky few could take advantage of some free instruction. Should a woman then pass an efficiency test her wage would be raised by 2s. a week.

In theory it sounded quite simple, but it was at the Selection Board stage that many willing recruits came to grief. The Selection Committee required references, which were discussed before a candidate's suitability was assessed. Many women were turned down without an interview, having first been judged on their ability to fill in a form or write a letter. According to the Selection Committees, it was very time-consuming to take up references before the applicant was seen, especially when the subsequent interview or medical examination proved that the woman was unsuitable. To examine references after the interview, and then to discover that the woman was ill-educated or unreliable would have been equally unsatisfactory. Those keen to get on with the job, and tired of being kept waiting, found employment through the Labour Exchanges, or privately. Many saw no reason to 'go official' at all and enlisted with one of the other recruiting bodies.

The 'Ladies on the Land', as they were dubbed by the *Daily Mail*, were still barred from most full-time agricultural colleges by virtue of their sex, and qualified women were scarce. Consequently, those who were promised training often had to fight for it. Women were still only beginning to ease their way into formal agricultural education, and, unlike the correspor.iing colleges for men, there were for them very few openings that offered a combination of both practical and technical instruction.

Under the direction of the Earl of Selborne, the Board of Agriculture had considered the whole question of agricultural education for women; indeed, whether it was actually worth paying for women to be trained, when the war might soon be over. Mrs Roland Wilkins wrote a number of reports on the subject in the *Journal* of the Board of Agriculture, which were later to prove of use to Rowland Prothero when he was appointed President of the Board in December 1916.

If parents were unhappy at the prospect of their daughters residing at predominantly male institutions there were no such worries at Studley College, to which

A Swanley girl carrying hay, c. 1918.
Millions of tons of hay were made during the First World War, most of it by hand.

women had been admitted for horticultural and dairy training since 1900, and where extra agricultural instruction was easily provided at the outbreak of war. Nor were there any problems at the unique Swanley Horticultural College which, since 1903, had admitted only women students. Elsa Morrow, author of 'Swanley Horticultural College 1889-1945', wrote:

> In 1914 it really seemed that student numbers were at the top; eighty-five for the start of the summer term. But the outbreak of war caused great uncertainty in the minds of staff and students alike, and numbers went down for a while. The Board of Agriculture was sending town girls, three at a time, who went straight into employment on farms, having spent three weeks learning milking and farm work.

In April 1915, Queen Mary visited the College, and handed over £100 'to assist in the work of training women of the professional classes who are suffering through the effects of the war.'

25

In Scotland, where, in 1911, a separate Board of Agriculture had been set up with responsibility for all matters relating to forestry and agriculture (with the exception of animal health); recruitment and allocation of women labour was undertaken by the Scottish Board, although much of the liaison work was carried out by members of the Women's Rural Institutes of Scotland. Here, one immediate effect of the war was that most of the male student members who had been elected as office holders at the Edinburgh College of Agriculture had enlisted by the beginning of the new year. In consequence, the unprecedented decision was taken to allow women into the Agricultural Society. According to the *Journal* of the College Former Students Association:

> The war did not end, some of those elected at that February meeting never returned, and the 1915-16 session opened with a girl on the Committee for the first time in the history of the Society. She was Margaret MacCallum who, with her sister, had been the first lady member to enrol.

Training

Lord Selborne had wished to see more women passing through the various county training schemes, and this was to provide the only solution in order to counter the opposition of farmers, who often complained of undisciplined enthusiasm on the part of women workers. However, until the formation of the Women's Branch, there was no single agency that could co-ordinate so substantial an increase in training facilities. Given a choice, most farmers would take a trained woman rather than one straight from a milliners; so trained women were much in demand.

In 1916, the President of the Board of Agriculture thought fit to insert the word 'training' in his message of persuasion:

> The army today, not perhaps so highly skilled, or so fully professional as the original Expeditionary Force, is none the less by dint of patriotism and zeal, a really magnificent army ... I am quite sure that if, with proper care and training, women can be given a similar chance in those classes of agricultural work for which they are fitted, that the assistance they could render to us will be proportionately great.

The Board also deliberated on the potential problems of men and women working together:

> If the man in the farmyard carried the food to the stock, the women could help to prepare the food, feed the young stock and milk; if the man weighs up the potatoes and loads up, the woman could riddle the potatoes ... at harvest time a man may drive the self binder, but the woman could stook the barley, oats and beans, and drive the horse and wagons better and more safely than a small boy; and three men and five or six women could staff a set of threshing tackle.

26

How many farmers followed this particular training schedule is not recorded, but women had already shown, both on the farms and in the cities, that they were no longer prepared merely to 'follow on behind'. The only way to improve their credibility was to allow them access to some real training.

Such instruction as existed in 1917 was provided by the county authorities, Local Education Authorities, Board of Agriculture agents, or agricultural colleges and farm institutes. In nearly every case it was a question of starting completely new courses for women or extending those that had existed for men. Some colleges put on courses of a few weeks duration for which the applicant paid, although these were later offered free of charge to legitimate WLA applicants. A list of courses was sent to the Board of Agriculture by the WACs or the education authorities, although many were set up and run by independent bodies, and often funded by private estate owners. The education authorities, local councils, and the Board, provided grants to help with the running of independent establishments, and the WACs were asked to co-operate in placing the graduates. Only WLA members signing on for the minimum of six months could expect to be offered training, and in some cases they were required to undertake work only in the county which had trained them. As this made it difficult to comply with their original commitment to go anywhere the WLA sent them, it was a stipulation impossible to enforce.

The Board required that courses should include milking, the feeding of calves, the current 'superior' methods of hoeing, and what was euphemistically described as the 'lighter' work of haymaking and general harvest duties. Since these courses were often crammed into a very short time-span, hundreds of 'trained' women were turned on to the land with only a vague idea of what was to follow: to be instantly disillusioned. Equally disillusioned farmers complained to the Board that whereas they had been expecting a competent employee, they had instead been landed with one they had to spend weeks 'breaking in'. In reality, women were often being asked to achieve in a few weeks what it had taken a male farmworker years to learn.

The courses varied in length from two weeks to two months. In Devon, the governors of the Seale-Hayne Agricultural College agreed to offer instruction and accommodation to fifteen students for a four-week course. In some counties selected farmers allowed students on to their farms for training. A pupil would be paid either directly by the local authority, or by the farmer, who, in turn, received a subsidy from the county. In Lancashire, the Education Committee arranged free courses of a month's duration for twenty-five students at the Hutton County Council farm. Some counties were unable to offer completely free instruction or accommodation, in which case, most were offered at nominal rates, and students allowed to earn small amounts while still technically being trained.

One of the more unusual forms of training was that provided by the mobile dairy schools in the Lake District, which charged an entrance fee of 2s. per student. The mobile dairy was one way of reaching remote districts, and it came within the scope of many women who might otherwise have been denied the opportunity to learn new skills. The van was fifteen foot by seven foot, with a thirty-foot long tent fixed to one side. It was able to accommodate fourteen students, and could be moved either by horse or by engine. An examination was held by the Principal of the Cumberland & Westmorland Farm School, at Newton Rigg, and certificates awarded to students. If any pupil was thought to be outstanding she would be considered for a scholarship at the Farm School.

Women who were given practical training on farms were generally housed nearby in a hostel or lodging. Those attending registered institutes or colleges led a more regimented existence. A typical example of this is the timetable for students attending the County Training & Clearing House Station at Elkington, near Louth, where twelve women at a time were given a two-week training course. Here, the students were looked after by a woman foreman, with accommodation provided free of charge for six of the women. Those on milking duty were to be at the dairy by 6.00 a.m., while the others would rise at that time, and after breakfast at 7 a.m., assemble for work at 7.45 a.m. Work commenced promptly at 8 a.m. and continued until midday, when there was an hour's break for lunch. Students were expected to help the matron prepare meals, and to take them to the workers who were in the fields or some distance from the farm. The afternoon work ended at 5.00 p.m., with a high tea provided at 5.45 p.m. Bedtime was at 9 p.m., and lights out at 9.30 p.m. precisely. Each student was responsible for the tidiness of her room, and also expected to take her turn in keeping the living quarters clean and comfortable.

At a training centre at Colton Bassett, in Nottinghamshire, on the estate of a Mr Knowles, the girls were taught to milk on 'The Artificial Udder'. A student would practice for up to an hour every day and then, it was hoped, be able to milk the real thing with comparative ease! A milk-training course, operated under the Hertford-shire WWAC, was carried out at local farms, although only two students were allowed to each farm, 'to save the cows from too large a number of prentice hands!'

At Swanley there were ninety-four students during 1916, many of them engaged on special War courses - in all subjects - which varied in length from five weeks to six months. One group of students, led by Dr Kate Barratt, was organised as auxiliary helpers in the flax factories. Situated as it was, in Kent, the Swanley students often went about their work to the sound of German Zeppelin's, or to the boom of the guns in France. All fruit and vegetable produce grown by the students at the college was marketed.

Many volunteers spent their training period on private farms, often in groups of three or more. A circular from the Board of Agriculture to the Womens' Committees and the Local Education Authorities, suggested that 'the farmer on whose land the women are to be employed should be asked to nominate one of his regular employees to act as instructor, and that a small payment of say 6d. a day should be made to the instructor from county funds.'

On the larger estates women were permitted to go about the farm with the usual staff, to pick up what they could, and then put it into practice. Hand-milking featured as the main undertaking but almost any farm task that needed doing, routine or

28

seasonal, was included. Unfortunately, this 'learn-as-you-go' practice often encouraged old retainers to delegate the less savoury jobs to the unfortunate girls, or for the wife of the owner to occupy the women with domestic rather than farm work.

On a five-hundred acre farm near Coventry, according to the *Journal* of the Board of Agriculture, the farmer, a Mr Vickers, took on eight girls, although only five stayed the course. He candidly admitted that he had applied for the women only because he was short-handed, and that he had not expected them to be much good. After only a few days, however, according to the report, he 'could not speak too highly of them.'

Many dutiful estate owners were to provide the training free, extending the scope of their patriotism to include board and lodging. Major and Mrs Peake were one such couple, and in May 1916 they set up the Bawtry Training Centre at their farm near Doncaster. Mrs Peake was secretary of the South Yorkshire WWAC, and had taken an active interest in getting women - educated women that is - on to the land. Mrs De Wilton was employed as instructor, and the course lasted two or three weeks. Regrettably, the centre was forced to close in its first winter owing to a shortage of applicants. Thatching was also taught at some centres, and Land Army members were the first to introduce a light muslin mask to wear as protection against the dust.

Inevitably, even in time of war, educated women were catered for in a completely different way to the untutored. No doubt many a capable, hardworking, village girl was denied the green armlet (the Board's symbol of service) because she was unregistered and poorly educated. Yet the possibility of combining brains and brawn is instanced by Olive Hockin in her book, *Two Girls on the Land*, published in 1918.

No experienced man exerts himself more than he needs ... a little strength exerted in the precise spot at the precise moment and he is far more effective than the exhausting efforts put forth by the uninitiated.

Miss Hockin learned to work and handle her horses 'as well as the next man', and grabbed the opportunity to prove a woman's worth with both hands: 'Looking around among the men I know, I can hardly think of one who would have stood one week of the work that we did.' A sentiment echoed by more than one Land Army woman!

In its *Notes on War Service for Countrywomen* the Board of Trade decreed that:

Women and girls of high standing socially . . . will at once learn to milk and will let the other inhabitants see them going, in suitable working dress, to and from their work day after day. Then their social inferiors will not be slow to follow their example.

It was this fine example, presumably, that the Board was after rather than any superior brain-power. Perhaps the absent men took as a compliment the implication that it required an educated woman to do their job for them! The extraordinary attitude that country people suffered from some kind of mental retardation which might possibly be contagious, was one that dogged many volunteers, and doubtless put off many applicants. The Government, it appeared, wanted both women who were intelligent, yet stupid enough to wish to do farm work! The prevailing attitude is perhaps exemplified in the question asked in Parliament on 21 November 1916. An MP wondered whether the reason for the closure of the Wiltshire WAC Training School might not be that the country and farm work 'grew too monotonous for town girls to put up with?'

The Parliamentary Secretary for Agriculture, the Rt. Hon. Francis Acland, informed the MP that the school had operated privately, and that closure had been brought about by its physical isolation during the war. His secondary comment, to

HARVEST HOME, 1918
WITH MR PUNCH'S JOYOUS CONGRATULATIONS TO THE MINISTER OF AGRICULTURE.
A typical *Punch* cartoon of the period, reproduced in *The Landswoman*, November 1918.

the effect that 'some few of the girls found the farm work too hard', served merely to fuel opinion that women were unable to cope with the demands placed upon them.

However, by the harvest of 1918, just about anyone, trained or untrained, would do. Following the German offensive in the spring of that year, the Government decided that 30,000 Grade I men, between the ages of eighteen and thirty-one, were to be conscripted before the 30 June. By the middle of June, it had become obvious that so serious a depletion of the workforce would mean sacrificing the harvest. In consequence, only 22,654 of the 30,000 men were called up, but replacement labour remained at a premium. Women were to be supplemented by prisoners of war, low-category soldiers, and war agricultural volunteers. Some one hundred and fifty members of the Metropolitan Police volunteered as ploughmen, and the number of public schoolboys, 5,000 of whom had helped to get in the 1917 harvest, was increased to upwards of 15,000.

Mechanisation

In one area of training, at least, men and women were placed on an equal footing: that of driving tractors. Here there were no time-honoured traditions. Both sexes came to mechanised farming together, although even here male prejudice may have prevented many women from reaching the driving seat. If the Board of Agriculture always had plenty to say on the subject of women and horses, it had few predictions about a woman's ability to handle a tractor. Possibly, for the Board's officials, it was an academic question!

The hurried introduction of tractors to British agriculture owed much to the urgent need to turn pasture over to arable, an exercise costly in terms both of labour and time. With traditional horse-power in short supply an alternative was urgently needed, and it arrived in the form of the internal combustion engine. In March 1917, the *Journal* of the Board of Agriculture stated that up to five acres a day could be ploughed, and six acres a day be cultivated, by the new machines. Most farm workers, however, knew nothing about this new form of tillage, and, as many of the older farmers refused to countenance these 'contrivances', it was very often the women volunteers who were left to take over the wheel and help to pioneer a revolution.

The Harper Adams Agricultural College, in Shropshire, was one of the first to offer courses for women mechanics. The Log, for the year ending September 1918, notes:

> At the request of the Food Production Department of the Board of Agriculture, courses of instruction were arranged in the autumn for the training of women in the driving and management of tractors. The Department provided the College with several makes of farm tractors, together with fuel and spare parts, and additional instructors were employed for the Course. The total number of women attending was 55.

In spite of the encouragement of the Board of Agriculture, however, the theoretical improvements in acreages ploughed per day could not be relied upon, nor maintained for very long periods, due to mechanical stoppages, inefficient handling, difficult soil conditions, and typically small or hilly fields. Tractors were also competing for vital fuel supplies. At the end of June 1917, the War Cabinet had instructed the Ministry of Munitions to arrange for the home production of 6,000 tractors to a specification that Henry Ford of Detroit had placed at their disposal; but their manufacture in wartime Britain proved to be impossible. It was, though, agreed to start their manufacture in America, and - the blockade allowing - to begin delivery in early 1918. Unfortunately shipping space remained at a premium for the rest of the war, and tractors never became a priority cargo. Even so, by 1917, the Government itself owned 477 machines, and had hired 135 from private owners. It even borrowed some 54 tracked vehicles or 'caterpillars' from the Russian government, although the archives do not indicate how this was achieved!

The Harper Adams initiative was, though, a success. The number of women in training at any one time varied from ten to twenty, and the period of instruction extended from six to eight weeks. During the evenings, lectures were given by the College Staff on the workings of the internal combustion engine, motor ploughs, or similar related topics. Practical instruction in driving and management was given on the College farm. All the women were sent by the Department of Food, and, as soon as they were considered to be competent drivers, they were directed to all parts of the country: from Buckinghamshire to Lancashire, and from Lincolnshire to the Isle of Wight. The women received excellent reports, one even rising to the position of Tractor Supervisor for her county, while others became Instructors. The weekly fee of 25s. per head was paid by the Department, and covered tuition, board, and residence.

Rallies

Those women who were successful in joining the WLA, or some other organised labour agency, still faced objections to their presence on farms from male workers.

Overcoming prejudice against women workers was still, in 1918, a priority for the Women's Branch. Following various demonstrations of women's work at shows in England and Wales, many farmers were won over, but many remained convinced that it would invariably take two women to do a man's job. The county shows were no longer a suitable vehicle to recruit members, or to demonstrate their work. A new idea was needed, and rallies became the vehicle of persuasion, and, literally, of demonstration.

On 29 January 1918, members of the Landworkers of Birmingham and Warwickshire marched through Birmingham. It was a day off for most, and everyone was exhorted to polish up boots and leggings. It was a glorious, spring-like day, and, wrote Doris Warden, in *The Landswoman*, 'Birmingham was full of jolly land girls, carrying the symbols of their work.'

> The procession attracted much attention, and to many of the watchers it was a novelty to see the girls in their working clothes, and to realise that the girls of England are really working on the land, and not merely playing about in print frocks in the haymaking time.

32

Efficiency certificates were presented to seventy of the eighty-four Warwick-shire and Birmingham girls present, some of whom had as many as six stripes.

The Great London Rally, held on 20 April 1918, was a further triumph. Over two hundred land women, headed by the band of the 17th Battalion London Regiment, and accompanied by flower-decked waggons, together with pigs, lambs and ducks, marched through the streets of the West End, and held a recruiting demonstration in Hyde Park. The procession began at the Food Production Department in Victoria Street at 10.45 a.m., and made its way down Whitehall, the Haymarket, Regent Street and Oxford Street to the YMCA headquarters in Tottenham Court Road. After lunch was taken at the Savoy Hotel the procession continued to Trafalgar Square, where the company dispersed to listen to the speeches. Miss Meriel Talbot gave a rousing address, and a deputation left for inspection by Queen Mary, at Buckingham Palace. An eyewitness account in *The Landswoman* reported:

> The rest of the day was spent in recruiting, magazine selling, and speech-making and hearing. It was a great reward for all our hard work - at the end of the day to be told that we had brought in 500 recruits and sold 5,000 copies of *The Landswoman*. I have since heard that as a result of the Rally 1,000 girls enrolled in the Land Army.

The Landswoman
Originally the journal of both the WLA and the Women's Institutes *The Land-swoman* started publication in 1918. It served as a friend to many an isolated Land Girl, and was intended to improve morale and provide a sense of corporate identity. *The Landswoman* was started by private enterprise, but edited and produced in London, at Blackheath, under the eye of the Women's Branch of the Board of Agriculture. It continued, until April 1919, as the joint publication of the Land Army and of the NFWI, but from that time was referred to as 'The Journal of the Land Girl and Every Country Woman'. The publication carried entertaining sketches on rural life, and numerous advertisements for suitable working clothes, including the notorious Liberty Bodice, which helped keep the winds at bay. It also carried regular reports of Rally News, and published photographs of marches and meetings, all contributed by readers. Cooking and gardening hints abound. There were regular competitions for essays, drawings, songs, and poetry, some of which earned prizes of between 6d. and 2s. News of the Recruiting Club was relayed breathlessly, so as not to be outdone by members of the Sewing Club, who revealed interesting ways of cutting out petticoats, and pooled their patterns of smocks, overalls, and camisoles. At the height of its circulation, cartoons from *Punch* were reproduced by 'special permission', although the magazine had demonstrated an extremely unsympathetic attitude to the role of women in the years before the war.

Placement

The *Journal* of the Board of Agriculture was quick to record instances of successful placements, and reported the triumphant success of women emerging from innumerable farms scattered throughout England and Wales. Every county had stories demonstrating a change in attitude on the part of the farmers as the war progressed. At a farm in Buckinghamshire, for instance, four women were employed: one from the early winter of 1915-16, and three from the early spring of 1916. Two were from London, one a teacher, the other a clerk. The first, though accustomed to country life, had done no farm work. Their main task was milking, cleaning the cowsheds, tending cows, as well as field work such as hoeing. Ten cows were milked at each session. The employer stated that at cleaning utensils, cowsheds, etc., the women were 'probably better than men', that they were most useful, and that the farm could not have carried on without them.

In Berkshire, a farmer employed two women, 'of the educated type', for eight months. Both from London, and with little training beforehand, their main work was, once again, milking and attending to the cows, plus some general farmwork, including work with horses. They also did a retail milk round in a nearby town. Their employer stated that at milking and cleaning-up the women do 'very well', and at the milk round they were particularly good - he did not know how it would have fared without them.

Three women in Devon were recorded as having pulled two acres of mangolds at 12s. an acre. The farmer afterwards said that he had been surprised at the quickness of the women, and was perfectly satisfied. Also in Devon, another four women pulled two acres of mangolds on the heaviest land in the parish for 14s. per acre, plus tea. Two of them did a quarter of an acre each day, and worked from 10.00 a.m. until 5.30 p.m., with an hour for lunch. The farmer said that the work could not have been bettered; and he probably said it with a smile, for it is likely that these enthusiastic war workers were more effective in time and money than his regular help.

The daughter of one Wiltshire squire went to work as a novice at a neighbouring farm, where she led a gang of women in providing useful labour. She first undertook docking in the wheat, and later played a considerable role in haymaking, and clearing out couch-grass, and other 'light work' - all this on top of the usual milking duties in the mornings and afternoons, and helping in the dairy generally.

Wages

Even after the setting up of the Wages Board in 1917 the question of wages, and conditions of work, continued to be a cause for unrest and complaint both from the farmer and the Land Girl. The Board of Agriculture did not help matters by announcing that wages would depend on the kind of work undertaken, the season of the year, and, to some extent, on the *relative capacity* of the individual woman. This last point was to prove the main problem. The Board was attempting to make the statutory wage less objectionable to the farmers, while encouraging cautious employers to take on inexperienced female labourers. It was also trying to appear fair to the Farmworkers Union, which had won a minimum wage for all workers - although it is unclear whether this had been intended to include women. There was, in the Wages Board settlement, no measurement for the quality of the work, only for the rate of pay. The Board knew that employers would feel resentful if they had to pay the new statutory rate to inexperienced women, but their refusal to pay was likely to make recruitment difficult for the WLA. The women themselves felt that, in most cases, their work was equal to that of the men, and that they should be paid accordingly. Women over the age of sixteen also expected employers to pay the new National Health Insurance contributions, which some employers managed to avoid by providing board and lodging. This exempted them from the 6d. employers contribution [the employee paid 3d.] as did employing itinerant or part-time workers, such as pea or hop-pickers, flower-pullers and onion peelers. The farmworkers' dilemma continued for some time. Should they accept equality of work and wages, or, under the circumstances, was it unpatriotic (not to mention unfair!) to object to alternative labour when, in fact, most of the women's work could not be faulted? Some reasoned that the women represented only a temporary extension of the part-time or seasonal work already done by village women, which role they would resume when the war ended. Traditionally, women's wages were lower than those for men, and it was hard for a man with a family to understand why a single woman should receive the same income as he did.

Initially, the Board of Agriculture stated that from 12-15s. a week might be considered an average wage for women 'under present conditions.' By March 1917, those enrolled in the Land Army would expect to receive a minimum wage of 18s. per week, rising to 20s. after three months, with an extra 2s. 6d. possible after a further three month's service. In 1919 some women were earning 25-30s. a week with various 'perks', such as railway passes, training, and maintenance during training, and the value of their uniform.

Uniform

The uniform, which the official government-appointed women and later the Women's Land Army members were expected to wear did not always assist their work. Women were expected to conduct themselves in a 'ladylike manner' at all times; a difficult stance to maintain in some farm situations!

The Board of Agriculture's approved costume consisted of a skirt, which was to come to within fourteen inches of the ground; a coat, reaching to the knees; a hat, of sou'wester design; boots with a Derby-cut front and weatherproof tongue; and leather leggings. In an official booklet, published in 1916, G.A. Greig stated:

Suitable clothing for women farm workers is important. I do not mean to infer that the garb need be picturesque, but rather that it should be dress of a fitting and useful kind, capable of protecting them from the ever-present dirt, and from the weather.

An advertisement from *The Landswoman*, November 1918,
representative of many which appeared in the magazine.

It was not picturesque; neither was it remotely practical; but it was certainly expensive. This unsuitable 'uniform' cost the woman worker around 30s., although it was understood by the Government that not everyone would need to buy the entire outfit from scratch. It was felt that most women would already possess some of the aforementioned articles of clothing, and for those who did not, it was suggested that employers would either help with the cost, or might at least advance the money and deduct it later.

In a circular letter sent from the Board of Agriculture to the WACs on 23 February 1916, it was proposed that the Women's Committees should consider raising funds locally for those women unable to afford to buy the costume. It suggested too that samples of the approved clothing should be supplied to the WWACs, who would then arrange further orders. Each was to have an Outfit Secretary and a Store Superintendent, both in a voluntary capacity. Elaborate bookkeeping and stock-taking was advised, to ensure that no waste or abuse took place. Orders for England and Wales were to be sent, with the cash, to the Co-operative Wholesale Society (CWS) in London, who would then forward the articles to the recognised committee. Unfortunately, in December 1916, the CWS advised the Board that owing to the increasing shortage of labour, and the difficulties in executing orders, it would not be possible for them to continue. They did agree, however, to clear the articles still in stock. The Board then advised the County Women's Farm Labour committees to assist women in procuring clothes suitable for land work locally, and at the most economical rate.

Naturally enough, opinions varied as to the suitability of the dress, although the women by no means all dressed according to official dictum. In 1918, the President of the Board of Agriculture, Rowland Prothero attempted to sound encouraging:

> There is nothing frivolous in instancing the admirable choice of the woman-like yet becoming uniform of the Land Army. Even Victorian prejudice grew reconciled to the dress or found solace in the reflection that it was very Greek.

By then, many of the women land workers had their own opinions on the practicality of the dress. One writer of an article that appeared in *The Landswoman* in 1918 saw the official uniform as a dubious sign of acceptance:

> It was not enough that women have worked steadily and faithfully . . . until they did it in uniform it was not noticed. When the Army had been efficiently nursed by the dance partner of pre-war days, now wearing a severe collar and an apron, they began to reconsider women; when the Board of Agriculture told the War Office - over a tall tumbler in a solemn club - how women could plough in smock and gaiters, the War Office, as a great favour, allowed a few pioneers to boil Tommy's potatoes.

The uniform could be issued to any registered woman who worked for more than twenty-four hours a week on the land. Other unofficial clothing, if no less inadequate, was on sale at every enterprising outfitters. Greens of Norwich considered it a matter of national importance that 'Lady Agriculturalists' be suitably attired, and advertised an assortment of farm overalls and weatherproofed coats. They also mentioned breeches - which though still unacceptable in most of the country, in Norfolk were worn quite early on in the war. The Hon. Lady Fellowes, speaking in July 1917 to the Norwich WWAC, said that their girls would be provided with an outfit, and, although it included breeches, she thought that there was 'nothing in the outfit to which the most particular person could take exception. It is a very pretty costume.' British land workers wanted to follow the lead of American women who, long before, in the person of Mrs Amelia Bloomer, had initiated the battle of the breeches. Even 'bloomers' were to be preferred to the long skirt. Only very gradually did practicality triumph against the opposition. A 'Special Correspondent' in London was finally able to write to her American readers:

> If anything could show how entirely different has become the attitude towards women's work in agricultural industry, in comparison with what it was in pre-war days, it is the evidence of dress . . . tunics or coats, knickerbockers, gaiters, thick boots and felt hats are the order of the day.

By 1918, Harrods was advertising a Farm Outfit, 'in good Genoa Corduroy, excellently cut jacket, button pockets, with convertible storm collar. The breeches button at the side with a buckle and strap at the waist. In dark brown only. All for 35s. 9d.' Harrods were also able to offer Service boots, specially constructed for farm work, and made on precisely the same principle as men's Army boots. These would cost the prospective Land Girl 37s. 6d!

Adding to the glamour of these outfits, was the armlet of green baize, bearing a red crown which, since March 1916, had been awarded by the President of the Board of Agriculture to any woman or girl over school-leaving age who had worked on the land for not less than thirty days since the commencement of the war. Distribution of the armlets was the job of the District Representative of the Women's Farm Labour committees, using the village correspondents when necessary.

The certificate issued with the armlet stated:

> Every woman who helps in agriculture during the war is as truly serving her country as the man who is fighting in the trenches, on the sea, or in the air.

3

Your Country Needs You!

Reminiscences of women on the land during the First World War.

Both animals and plants are largely dependent on the weather, and as this cannot be forecasted with any certainty it is impossible to keep to any rigid programme of operations. The work of the day must be settled on the day itself and on the spot; everything later can be provisional only and subject to the condition: weather permitting. This habit of making daily decisions engenders a spirit of independence of mind and judgment often mistaken by superficial observers for obstinacy.
Sir John Russell, English Farming, *1942*

At the outbreak of the First World War, I was living in the Wye Valley, nearly seventeen and rather idle. But, my father being abroad, I was the daughter to stay at home. This happy, but perhaps useless, existence came to an end one August evening, with a telegram delivered by a village boy. I, and everyone else, awoke. The call for women was, I think, not immediate, except for the nursing profession; but gradually pressure built up, and, even in the then very remote countryside, one felt the urge to help. I was what was known as an 'outdoor' girl, and the Land Army attracted me; but I thought I should be more useful if I had some real knowledge and training.

Reading University was offering courses of three to four months to prepare girls for land work, and it was arranged that I should do this. We lived in St. Andrew's Hall, which was the only Women's Residential Hall then, and my memories are very pleasant. We learned dairy work, butter and cheesemaking, milking cows (by hand), and received lectures on the welfare and care of stock. I can't remember much about poultry, but it *is* a very long time ago, although I do remember many pleasant weekends on the river!

39

However, at the end of this period, we did not join the Land Army but an organisation called The Women's Farm and Garden Union. Through this we were offered work. I think now the old bugbear of class distinction must have been at work, but I was far too naïve to realise anything of this, and I went happily down to Sussex to the estate of a Liberal MP. His wife was very active in working for Womens Rights, and quite advanced for the times. The bailiff of the estate was a woman - very efficient and capable; and she directed our work, but otherwise left us entirely to live our own lives. There were four of us permanently, and we were allocated three cottages on the estate, fairly modern and pleasant, but with no sanitation, and the loo to each one in the garden. Twice a week we could have a bath up at the House. This sounds incredible now, but it was by no means unusual then, and caused no complaint. I was the dairymaid; there was the carter, who worked in the stables; the chaffeuse (for the one car); and a fourth girl, who worked in the fields at seasonal work, and in the gardens.

I worked under the cowman. There were about ten cows, which I had to fetch in from the fields, and chain up in the cowshed by 7.00 a.m.... The milk was set in large round pans on slate slabs which lined the dairy walls, and at night I skimmed off the cream for butter-making, and for use in the house. I do not think I ever had a separator then, but they were beginning to be used. Having done the immediate dairy work, I went back to the cowsheds, to help the cowman clean down the sheds, to cut hay from the rick, and put it ready in the racks for the night feed, and to feed any young calves that were being weaned. Twice a week I churned cream into butter for the house, and also kept them supplied with soft cheese.

It is difficult to describe the farming of 1914-18. It is so utterly changed that I have no interest in looking round a farmyard now. Our farmyard was square, with the cowsheds one side and the stables facing us; the centre was a dung heap (not as unpleasant as some silage now). The dung was removed to the fields and spread, and sometimes that job was done by us, though usually by the men. It was extremely heavy work, as anyone knows who has moved a fork-full of dung from one place to another! Two of us - standing on the dung heap - loaded the cart, and another led the horse away to the field. There the dung was unloaded in reasonable heaps, in lines across the field, to be spread later.

I cannot describe as I should like, the farm men we worked with. Very real countrymen, slow and gentle. I never remember bad language, though admit to not always following the Sussex dialect. I hope they respected us, as we respected them. I shall always remember Dixon, the carter, calling me across to the stables one dark morning to have a cup of tea in the harness room with him and his mate. That the tea tasted of paraffin and horses meant less than nothing. I had been accepted into a Holy of holies, and I was then allowed to help harness Blossom, as he lowered his lovely head to thrust through the collar I help up to him. I am an old woman now, but I find it is these things I remember.

We had, should I say, no amusements; and there was the almost constant sound of [the] guns from France. Every so often a face would be gone from the table, and a whisper go around of bad news from France. Sometimes this face would appear again, and work continue as usual. Yet we were happy, and I look back upon it as a time of great friendships and growth that I would not have missed. The sad and bitter thing is that we thought we were helping to win the last ever war. The war to end all wars.

Betty Farquhar, Inkberrow, Worcestershire.

I was still at school when the war started. Although not of farming stock (my father being a doctor) I had been brought up surrounded by animals of all descriptions - horses, dogs, rabbits, and such. I knew early on that I wanted to farm, and persuaded my parents to allow me to apply for a course in agriculture. In those days there was no free access to such institutions for women, and those colleges that existed had only men students. But I had heard that there was to be a women's agricultural college founded - Cheltenham, I think - and I wanted to be part of it. Being an only child, and I suppose rather spoilt, my father agreed.

Two friends were equally keen and, in 1915, we heard that a Mrs Watson Kennedy was taking girls on to her farm. The training would be six weeks, and we thought: what can anyone learn in six weeks? We had to pay for the training, but the three of us set off in my Ford Flivver. We did the six weeks, and then both my friends left. Mrs Kennedy said I could stay and work on the farm. Luckily the cowman was nice, and would teach me anything I wanted to learn. Women had only worked at certain jobs on farms in those days, like field work, and not many worked with animals or in dairies. Living in rural Norfolk, as I did, I was not associated with any womens' movement, and I lived a very isolated life. If there were newspapers, I never saw them. I just wanted to get on to the land. I think a new branch of the WI was being started in the village, but I never went to a meeting as it was several miles from home, and once work started I had no time. There was no *Landswoman* magazine where I was, and no official war-work organisation.

Mrs Kennedy had the first Jersey attested herd in England, and I desperately wanted to work with the cows. Everyone had said the Norfolk marshes were too harsh for Jerseys, but they were not. One girl was already working in the dairy. We got up at 5.00 a.m., and rarely had any time off at all. I had my keep, and five shillings a week, and I loved it! There was a man who drove the milk cart, but when he left I was asked whether I would take it on. I still kept on four of the cows, and added my milk round at Blakeney. Half a pint of Jersey milk then sold for a penny three farthings! I walked the round, and was home for breakfast before 9.00 a.m., then fed the pony. After lunch, there was the second milking to do, and numerous other work. Cows always seem to like calving at night, and I used to sit up sometimes - first with the cowman, and then alone. The very first time I did this, it was twins. The cowman was horrified, the next morning, that I had not sent for him.

I got married before the end of the war - my husband a boy of nineteen in the trenches, never having held a rifle in his hand; not even to shoot a rabbit. I moved

41

Dorothea Cross.

to a farm in Northrepps where I was able to get leave at twenty-four hours notice, in case I needed it. There I did the milk round into Cromer, with a funny little pony named Snowball who used to round up the cows. We had Shorthorns there, but they were not so nice after my dear Jerseys.

I heard there about the new WI movement; but I was always too busy, and the village was a long way from the farm. I wore a smock for most of the war, but towards the end we had visits from the official Land Army, who were dressed up in hats and breeches. We had no contact with any unions, and there were no rallies or recruiting drives.

Dorothea M. Cross, Swardeston, Norfolk.

In 1915, some Co-operative Farming people canvassed the Colleges for help with fruit picking . . . Newnham volunteered, and the terms were, that accommodation would be provided but we would have to 'do' for ourselves. We would be paid 15s. a week for normal hours, but go on to 'piece' rates when the fruit was plentiful.

We lived in Jephson Hall - on the Sutton Bridge to Lynn road. The Hall was divided into two main sections, with the back one divided again into two small rooms: one for our Leader, who was a Tutor, and the other into a Wash Room, with eight tin basins on trestle tables, and a jug of boiled water for teeth. Our water came from a small rain well and was used very sparingly, as it had to last the whole summer. There were two long trestle tables, and a small cooking stove, in the other section at the back of the Hall.

The front of the Hall contained our ticking mattresses (which we filled with straw on arrival) on the floor. I remember that by the second night there was not a shoe among the company which did not witness to the mortality of the apparently usual inhabitants, the beetles.

We were a group of fifteen souls, with a rota of thirteen workers and two housekeepers. Baths were a difficulty. The local doctor allowed us two a day in his house, but the boiler burst the next winter, so he could not keep that up. The local pub let us have two a day at a cost of 3d. each, and for those who could get into Lynn under their own steam [there was] the Globe Hotel. I hired a bike for 2s. 6d. a week.

Sir Richard Winfrey was our planner, and he came down to see us installed, and sent the Press later on. We were officially in the Women's National Land Service Corps and wore khaki armlets till we qualified by length of service for green baize ones with a red crown. I still have them both. We had no uniform, and wore gym slips or overalls. The plan joined us with a bunch of regular village women, who treated us at first with distinct caution if not actual disdain. But we wore them down with our tomfoolery, and we sang lots of songs with good choruses. The main one was 'The American Railway' with a chorus of 'Patsiooria' and so we became called by that name.

The farm was some miles away, so bikes were a necessity. Our hours got caught up with the beginning of Daylight Saving. For example, the first year we picked strawberries and got them on the early train to London for lunch. The next year with the hour difference, the berries were not right for picking to do that. But we were still up by 6.30 a.m., to a mug of milk and dry bread - and no washing! We rode to the farm and worked until 8.30 a.m., and rode back for a breakfast of porridge, bread and honey. Back at 9.30 a.m. until 12 noon, when the housekeeper came with bread and cheese (no butter), and we got tea from the farm. If funds were good we maybe had roast potatoes or sausages. We worked again from 12.30 p.m. to 4.00 p.m., and back for a supper of soup, potatoes and rice, and a wash, and bed - officially - around 8.00 p.m. The first week we had to buy the odd pan, etc., and our wages were down to a ½d. each. We all trooped down to the nearest shop, and spent the lot!

The local folk were most kind. The doctor took a great interest in us, and I kept up a good friendship with him and his family, and visited them for as long as I can remember. Other people invited two or three of us each weekend for a meal, and a look at civilisation again. I remember one lady who was good to us: she had twenty-four rabbits, lots of pigeons, three hives of bees, two greenhouses, and a motor bike!

The Press came down with its cameras; and articles appeared in the local and the Cambridgeshire newspapers. One article was headed 'The Princess in Real Life', and [went on] 'their hoods were bewitchingly rural and only their speech betrayed them, for they came from Newnham.' Photographs were many. Typical stuff, showing rows of us with hoes over our shoulders; bunched on a hay bale with mugs of tea and buns; crouched over the strawberry rows, and so on. But the main one was of all of us sitting cross-legged down the farm track with our hands clasped behind our heads. This was reproduced on the large shop posters in Cambridge in full size with the indignant caption - 'Is this what higher education does for women?' Remember, we lived in a time when no woman wore trousers!

Hilda Rountree, Uppermill, Oldham.

I was staying with friends in Netley, Hampshire, when I decided to join the force of women volunteering to work on the land. I had already learned to hand milk (extremely slowly), but that was about all. I knew that I loved animals and the countryside, and wanted so much to do something useful. Men were volunteering for war service, and I could think of nothing more suitable than helping to keep the country fed.

I knew little or nothing about the womens' movements going on in the towns. We country women thought the suffragettes scatter-brained individuals. The WI movement had started to establish itself, but although I did join later, I had little time, from 1916 until the war ended, to bother with such things. Institutes were founded and flourished in the early war years, though it was unfortunate that many women who would have been its staunchest members found it impossible, either from pressure of work or sheer isolation, to support its establishment. I did join the Women's Farm and Garden Union in 1916. My certificate of enrolment for land work is dated May 1916, and was signed both by Mr Walter Runciman, President of the Board of Trade, and Lord Selborne, then President of the Board of Agriculture. It is very grand and patriotic, as I suppose it all was then.

My first job lasted the best part of a year. I worked for Mr Thomas Fry of Westover Farm, Ringwood in Hampshire. I remember my Boss told me that when I could comfortably hand milk eight cows I could think I was taking the place of one man. There was a lot to prove in that first month, but I did learn to milk many more than eight cows at a sitting. I remember a joke that was played on me when I was new, and I suppose on lots of other girls. There was one cow who was separated from the rest as she had recently calved. I used to take the calf out at intervals and milk the mother. One morning I went as usual to the box, and thought nothing of the tittering going on in the cowshed. When I opened the door, there, instead of the cow, was the bull. By that time I was aware of the difference, and made myself scarce!

In those early days we were not issued with a uniform, although I think some were later. It was still customary for women to wear long skirts, whether doing farm work or not. I rigged myself up with a shorter than usual skirt, a shirt, and an old black slouch hat. We often had to collect animals from the station, perhaps bullocks that the farmer had bought, and quite often there was some chasing to be done on the way home. The station was about two miles from the farm, and the animals were often bewildered and nervy after their journey. One particular day there was more running about than usual. In Chapel that Sunday, horrified tales were circulating about a woman running around the town in a short skirt - 'so short yer could see her *britches*!' I had to admit that the woman was myself, and explained, I think in vain, about the need for more suitable work clothes. We were later issued with some official uniform, and, later still, with breeches. The skirts were so impractical it was little wonder that men thought women would not be able to cope. I don't suppose they would have coped, if *they* had been made to wear skirts down to their heels!

I did not regard the work as a job, more a way of life; which was just as well, since we got very little time off. When I finished in the cowshed there was field work, and in the winter the threshing party would come round and turn the farm upside down for a few weeks. I do not think many of the men were at odds with me because I was female, but there was one horseman who resented my being allowed to drive the pony and buggy into town, and refused point-blank to harness up for me. So I did it myself, and, so long as the boss approved, he never put his objections into words - just silently made clear his disapproval of such goings-on.

Later on in the war, one of the county organisers persuaded me to start teaching farming skills. I arrived at one farm where there was already a local woman helping to milk. I remember the filth, and the nonchalance with which she worked. She wore a man's cap turned round the wrong way so that she could lean comfortably into the cow's side when milking, and a long skirt which trailed in the mud and muck. The cowshed was disgusting, and hygiene unheard of. Nobody thought very much about the 'whys' and 'wherefores' of keeping dairies clean. I determined then that I would do my bit to bring about a change on that farm at least, and blessed Mr Fry for his good training and common sense at Ringwood.

One training technique we had for milking was an 'automatic cow'. It consisted of a canvas bag on four legs, complete with four rubber teats. The bag was filled with water, and the teats adjusted by screws to allow hard or easy milking. I suspect it was as valuable in terms of merriment as it was in practical instruction.

We had very little social life in those days. There was a small community hall in the village, and visiting players used to come and put on a variety of theatrical performances. There were whist-drives too, but I could seldom get away, especially in winter. I remember one farm where the milk from the herd used to go to the station. We had a cart pulled by mules, which could be very stubborn. The milk had to be at the station by 7.30 a.m., loaded up in seventeen-gallon churns. They were too heavy to lift, so we had to roll them and watch out for the tops. I often had to seek a helping hand from someone because of the ice. The mules had to be led from the farm, and we all slipped and slid our way uneasily to and from the station. And this was after getting up, long before dawn, staggering through the dark and cold, milking, and loading the churns before seven in the morning!

Beatrice Oaks, Diss, Norfolk

[After the War, Miss Oaks obtained a training scholarship, and went on to become an Instructress at Swanley College. She was a lifelong member of the Women's Farm and Garden Association, and trained many Land Girls for work on farms during the Second World War.]

I joined the Land Army in 1918, and stayed in it for some years. I joined, soon after leaving school, against my parents wishes, because I had always wanted to live in the country (I was a Londoner), and loved animals.

My experiences were very mixed: some good, some bad. I was stationed first in Buckingshamshire, and afterwards in Surrey. Mostly my work [consisted of] dairy work, milking, looking after calves, and some field work.

At Dorney, in Buckinghamshire, I shared a cottage with three girls, and we did all the milking - ten cows each - twice a day. We had to look after ourselves, and, of course, get up very early. This was my happiest time. Also in Buckinghamshire, two other girls and myself shared a cottage on a Duke's estate, which was terrible: only the bare necessities of life, and about ten yards from some abandoned pigsties which housed a few hundred rats! Before we could have even a cup of tea we had to collect wood to light a fire.

Apart from milking, I had to take the milk and a float to Gerrards Cross every day. While in Reigate, I did a milk round.

Dora Brazil, Seaton, Devon.

Wishing to help the war effort, I took a three-month gardening course in Gloucestershire, in 1918. Garden produce was sold locally. The student in charge of the horse and cart had a real performance to harness the animal and had to stand in the manger; once in the cart the horse was reasonably manageable. The winter months [during which] I was at the College were cold, and the ground frozen deep. We used to hack potatoes the size of marbles, and measly parsnips, out of the ground. So bad was the food problem ... [that] customers were glad even of those. After the course, I did not join the Land Army but was directed to Leicestershire, to the Hunting Box of the 'Coats Cotton' family. For a time I lodged with the wife of the butler, who was at the war. The gardening staff included two elderly men, too old for active service; a girl from the village pub, and a Scottish lass, all under the charge of the Head Gardener. Unfortunately, I had very bad colds, and at these times I was sent to the Rectory, in the village, where I received great kindness always; but such was the food problem that when, at supper, we were literally offered 'porridge mould', it was accepted gratefully!

It was my job to look after the boiler fires at night. These heated five or six greenhouses. I used to visit them at 11.00 p.m., as the fires were very temperamental, and there was trouble if the houses cooled off. The walk to the gardens [took] a lonely fifteen minutes, but one had no fear of walking alone in those days. After a time Mrs Coats arranged that the Scots gardener and myself should live in the bothy, which, with grooms and gardeners away, was vacant. A dear old soul walked from a neighbouring village to cook our breakfast and midday meal. Rations were so inadequate that we were very dependent on the vegetable produce and milk allowed us, with an occasional old hen given to us by our employer.

In the winter months, I seemed to spend my time wheeling barrows of manure for the two men, until Mrs Coats saw me at this work and said she wanted to try to wheel the barrow. To her mind the work was too heavy for a girl! There was always plenty of work to be done in the greenhouse, as Mrs Coats liked plenty of flowers for the house. The Head Gardener, and Sandy, the Scottish lass, spent hours each morning with flower decoration. In the summer, I mowed from 6.30 a.m. to 5.30 p.m. with a mowing machine, small for such a large area of lawn. I had a Shetland pony with overgrown hoofs, and the other girl gardener pushed the machine.

I recall the heavy work, planting and harvesting potatoes in a field away from the main garden. The wife of the remaining groom used to bring out a tray of tea and scones to refresh us - and how thankful we all were for this respite. One particular day we were told to rake the front drive for guests, and we watched their arrival through the bushes. I recall two or three children; one fair boy of about six, who is now the present Duke of Wellington. My Scottish friend Sandy and I remained friends, with letters and visits to each others homes, from 1918 to 1977, when she died. I need no pat on the back for the fact that, at knocking-off time, [at 5.30 p.m.], if a piece of work I had set out to do was not finished I always stayed on to complete the job ... My wage was 18s. per week, and I believe my lodgings were paid for. It was not until I left, that my employer told me that she ought to have negotiated for her girl gardeners instead of leaving arrangements to the Head Gardener. I had a taste of the 'servants hall': they did not want us to eat with them - the cook, lady's maid, head housemaid, and parlour maid - and definitely let the housekeeper know this. We had our own rooms and helped with cooking in the bothy. After a time in Leicestershire, I felt that my time was not being spent on work of necessity, so I sought other fields - in the YMCA on Salisbury Plain.

Edith Hedworth, Atworth, Melksham, Wiltshire.

I worked on the land as a member of the Women's Land Service Corps, which was started and organised by the Women's Farm and Garden Union. I trained for about six weeks at a large Estate belonging to Lady Fitzgerald of Buckend House, near Faringdon, in Berkshire. She was rather an alarming lady, and used to ask us to tea with her at the Mansion, two at a time, on Sundays. Food at that time was not too plentiful, so an elegant afternoon tea was appreciated as an extra.

Enrolment of Land Army girls, c. 1915-16.
A photograph taken at Mr J. Thisleton-Smith's farm at West Barsham, Norfolk.
Miss Burton-Fanning presents an armband to a cook/dairymaid.

We were taught, by going with her usual farm staff, to handle the horses, plough, harrow, and to milk by hand a herd of small black Kerry cows with tiny udders and teats. About eight of us, aged seventeen to twenty-four, lived in a sparsely furnished house in Buckland village run by a very pretty Scotswoman. At the end of our course, she helped arrange the jobs for us to go to. Mine was as junior carter at Mr Stratford's Bosmore Farm, at Fawley, near Henley-on-Thames, where I worked from the spring of 1918 to the summer of 1919.

I lived with two other girls in a tied cottage, [and] an old woman nearby cooked our supper. We had to walk up a hill - about half a mile, to reach the stables, and get there by 6.30 a.m. We fed the horses in their stalls, then had a snack breakfast, heating cocoa on a tiny stove. We groomed and harnessed up, and were at work in the fields by 8.00 a.m. Around 10.30 a.m. we had a break for 'Nuncheon'. We carried our food, tied up in red cotton handkerchiefs, in a woven straw hod that hung easily on the harness. Back to the stables by 3.00 p.m. we fed, watered, and groomed the horses, mucked out the stalls, racked up with hay for the night, and knocked-off work at 5.00 p.m. No half-day on Saturdays, and a starting wage of 18s. a week, paid and signed for every Friday afternoon. Free lodgings; wood, coal, and oil for the lamps.

There were four teams of plough horses. The head carter was a nice man. He lived close to the farm with his wife and three little daughters. A good teacher, he took a real interest in our progress.

The farmer rode a pony called Peacock, and would arrive suddenly in the field to see how the work was progressing. On one occasion he remarked, 'Now then, you great strong men, don't stand there all day with your hands in your pockets up to your elbows!'. As a retort, when he one day offered to help with a heavy loading job, the head carter said under his breath, 'Yes, you push and I'll grunt'! Mr Stratford sometimes lent us his trap, a governess-cart, for a Sunday afternoon drive. Besides Peacock, there were two skewbald ponies - Lily and Daisy. Abbott, the foreman, sometimes rode them. He looked after the cow and the poultry.

During my time at Bosmore I learned to plough a straight furrow. I had various teams - Tiny and Blossom, Violet and Diamond. These last two were cast Army horses - not true cart horses like those of the head carter, Sergeant and Boy. They were most intelligent; as was Count, a huge obstinate Liver Chestnut.

The farm was on flinty chalk, with not much level ground, and about 300 acres.

We had a house cow, but no dairy herd, and no pigs. There were sheep, managed by Shepherd Barnett and the odd-man Derrick. They used to spend a lot of time penning the sheep on the root fields. 'One pushes totherun, totherun pushes back, and down go the hurdles, look see', Derrick used to say. The sheep were sheared at the farm by two itinerant shearers, and we loaded a big waggon with the wool, which then went to Wallingford; for that, our horses always had on the best harness, with shining brasses and bells on their headpieces.

At haymaking, Alice - the maid of all work - in a long dress of blue cotton, with a white apron, used to help by leading the horses on the waggon as it started off to the next row of haycocks. She called 'stand firm, pull up', to the carter on top of the load and to the horses. One of the girls had rather well-cut breeches (mine were old Army ones of my brothers), and Mr Stratford said to her: 'I wish you'd give the name of your tailor to the others'. It was a pleasant break to take a horse to be shod at Fawley village, up another hill. The blacksmith's wife always asked us into her house for a cup of tea while the job was being done.

We never penetrated into the farmhouse. I think Mrs Stratford was 'delicate', and a recluse. The work was physically hard, but we got used to it. When very tired, in bad weather, I sometimes wished that my war work was in an office or under cover! But I enjoyed it. The early walk up the hill, with glorious sunrises, the outdoor life of field and hedge; the comradeship; the satisfaction of doing a good job, with the co-operation of one's horses; the fun of our own cottage. Baths took place weekly in a brick-floored lean-to scullery. To heat up the water we used to light a fire, usually of gorse twigs, under the old-fashioned copper, and then bale the hot water into a metal bath, and finally tip the bath in the right direction so that the contents flowed out through a gap in the wall. Our drinking water we drew from a well, and the 'loo' was an earth closet, in a shed in the garden!

This experience, though it lasted only two years, gave me a lifelong interest in farming. I can remember now the fertilizer we used on the farm: it was Basic Slag - a grey powder with a fearful smell - which we fetched in sacks from Henley!

Anne Farewell-Jones, Sidmouth, Devon.

4
The Intervening Years

After the Land Army was disbanded in 1919, many of the members took advantage of the free passage to the Dominions offered to ex-service men and women. Others continued in farm or garden work at home, or became farm owners themselves. Many married countrymen, and doubtless a large number returned to their former occupations.

Dame Meriel Talbot, DBE

Hostilities ceased at 11.00 a.m. on 11 November 1918, and only just in time. Conditions boded ill for the harvest. Morale was low and resources stretched to their limit. The spring target of drawing 30,000 Grade I men into the fighting services had severely crippled agriculture, and disillusionment was rife not just at home but amongst servicemen. A feeling had crept in that women, by taking on men's work, were unwittingly prolonging the war. John Terraine, in *Impacts of War 1914 & 1918*, cites a soldier in the 17th Division, who wrote home:

> Good Luck I say to anyone who can keep out of this hell. I am surprised that you have joined the WLA. Do you realise Maggie you are helping to prolong the war? I suppose you did not think. What does it matter whether we win the war or not? We shall never get it over so long as the women and girls keep relieving men for the Army . . . only when there are no men left will the war finish, that is the way the lads look at it out here.

Maggie, and others like her, had found themselves in an impossible situation. The Newnham women had been berated by an indignant Press; what would the reaction have been had they not rallied to the Call?

It is astonishing that so many had been willing to accept the often appalling living and working conditions involved in keeping the nation fed. Not for the Land Army the companionship of the other women's services. Instead they were asked to accept low pay, a pitifully inadequate uniform only grudgingly given, and, for some, an unfamiliar isolation within a rural community which seemed to belong to

51

another age. The idyllic vision of rural Britain has always been popular with propagandists in time of war. Once the women arrived, and were confronted with the reality, it was often only pride that kept them in service. Theirs was a necessary but largely unspectacular heroism, and although some stayed, because they were still required or had made their homes there, the rest, released after four years to get on with their lives, returned to their homes and found a changed society.

The image of the 'New Woman' of the pre-war years, enhanced by war service, now needed overhauling. As early as 1915 *Punch*, instead of lampooning women's aspirations to independence had taken to championing them, and, during the war years, women had benefited from this new perception. As Deirdre Beddoe in *Discovering Women's History* put it:

Magazines, posters, films and paintings depicted the new desirable stereo-type. She was 'the girl behind the man behind the gun' - the 'munitionette', the VAD or the landgirl. Propaganda films deplored the old pre-war life of idleness of the middle-class woman and praised the rigours of life in the land army.

As four million men were demobilised, and put back on the job market, women found their prospects for employment severely diminished. Jobs that they had taken with such speed under the 'Right to Serve' banner were no longer theirs, even though they were jobs that they had proved more than capable of doing. Half a million of them claimed unemployment donation at the start of 1919 but by the end of the year the champions of the 'Home Front' found that there was little alternative but to return there. Was the argument still that a woman not forced to work was taking the bread from a man who was? Were women really to be trampled underfoot in the rush of returning farm workers?

The effects of the war on agriculture continued to be felt well into the 1920s. The dire shortage of foodstuffs meant that women land workers were among the last to leave the service of their country. Although the new programme, drawn up in the spring of 1918, to increase the arable acreage of England and Wales by one million acres, was never submitted to the Cabinet for decision, the enormous task of the national harvest was still crucial. The Board of Agriculture decided against enforcing the new compulsory ploughing orders, and expressed the hope that improvements in yield might still come from the existing tillage.

The waning of political interest in agriculture during the 1920s matched the realities of peace, and marked an end to the nation's short-lived gratitude for home food production. The appalling weather during the 1918 harvest had put paid to the forecasts of high crop yields, and had left farmers with a barely adequate return for all the planning. This, which had the war not ended might better have been described as a disaster, failed to bring home to politicians the nature of farming, and its necessary philosophy: 'no yield is a true one until the barn door is firmly closed upon it.' No amount of government direction can feed a nation in the face of inclement growing conditions. Members of the War Cabinet may have come to terms with the losses from submarine attacks but they were frustrated, to say the least, by incessant August and September rains. Temporarily frustrated that is, since it was clear to the most humble of Britain's farmers that the solution lay in a resumption of imports.

Guaranteed prices for wheat and oats had gone some way towards helping farmers maintain sufficient prosperity to stay in business, and to begin with it did seem as if the future of Britain's countryside would be more cheerful than it had been for some time. From January 1920, agriculture was to be served by a new Ministry of Agriculture based on the existing Board of Agriculture. All departments, except for forestry - which was to come under the newly-established Forestry Commission - were united under one roof embracing all those wartime activities that had not reverted to the Board of Trade and which in some way had to do with food. It may well be significant that this move came about as the result of a Private Member's amendment, rather than through the initiative of the Government. The Food Production Department was wound up in March 1919, although the Ministry of Food functioned until 1921, when its few remaining duties reverted once more to the Board of Trade.

During those early post-war years the sun shone briefly in the form of the Prime Minister, David Lloyd George, who had solemnly promised that his government would not forget farming, nor the women's role and its contribution to the war years. Mrs Pankhurst had continued to give her unqualified support to the war effort and to the Prime Minister. On the 11 January 1918, women over the age of thirty - with some qualifications - were given the right to vote. 'Women's Rights' took the place of 'Votes for Women'. Initially, six million women were enfranchised - but they first had to be returned to their firesides from the factories, and from the land, to take up where they had left off.

The army of women which had served the nation in the turnip fields and cowsheds, felled timber, and guarded forage dumps, was now to be disbanded. *The Landswoman* announced that Princess Mary, the only daughter of George V and Queen Mary, had been invited to the Drapers' Hall in London, on 27 November 1919, to present the Distinguished Service Bar to fifty-five members of the Land Army. A photograph of the Princess, taken especially for the magazine, featured in the special Christmas issue, a copy of which was given to all 250 women who attended. The programme opened at 5.30 p.m., with supper at 7.15 p.m., followed by a concert which included Morris and clog dancing, recitations, songs, and a violin solo. The Lord Mayor was present, together with the last President of the Board of Agriculture, Lord Lee, and Mrs Roland Wilkins, who had been responsible for throwing the resources of the Women's Farm and Garden Union behind the establishment of the Women's National Land Service Corps. Mrs Wilkins, the first woman to read for an agricultural degree at Cambridge University, was to work continually and enthusiastically for practical agricultural education for women both during and after the war. The recently enobled Lord Ernle, and Lady Ernle, were also in attendance. Lord Ernle, as Rowland Prothero, had presided over the Board of Agriculture from 1916 until September 1919.

The Times described the occasion in full, calling it one of the 'prettiest ceremonies the City has ever seen'. The best plate of the Drapers' Company gleamed in the modern electric lighting which illuminated pictures of all the monarchs from Charles II to King Edward VII. The girls were apparently 'gallant looking', in their white overalls and 'gay little hats'. They also wore corduroy breeches, which had by then won some respectability. Each woman wore a crimson carnation in her buttonhole, and bore the sleeve badge of the Land Army. Flowered wands, loaned by the Lady Mayoress, were held to make an avenue for the Princess when she arrived. While the company was settling down for the presentations the girls sang their rallying cry:

> Come, lasses and lads,
> Take leave of your Dads,
> And away to the country hie.

Miss Meriel Talbot, of the Women's Branch, was on hand to announce each member as she was presented to the Princess. One award caused a particularly rapturous welcome as the girl had saved the life of a man being gored by a bull. An unromantic beginning possibly - but the girl had gone on to become his wife!

The Princess, known to dread public appearances, had nevertheless given her practical support and encouragement to the various women's war groups. In what was her first public speech, she said:

> The war work of the women and girls of Great Britain will always be gratefully remembered by their King and country. I have watched with much interest the origin and growth of the Land Army, and today I realise more than ever all that it has accomplished, and what skill and courage have on many occasions been displayed by its members . . . I congratulate the President of the Board of Agriculture and the Women's Branch on the work they have done, and I wish you all every happiness in the future.

The Times reported Lord Lee's speech, including his comment, 'Of all classes of women employed during the war you were one of the worst paid'; a sentiment that the girls, and the Princess, warmly applauded. He believed that there was a future for many of them on the land, but all he had been able to obtain from the Treasury was the promise that any remaining members of the Women's Land Army should have a new outfit. This was not a bad deal for the Treasury, as most of the girls had bought their uniform with their own money.

The dinner marked the end of the nation's requirement for women to take the place of men in the matter of food production. Just when the whole business of administration seemed to have achieved some degree of effectiveness it was all over. A note in the Harper Adams record book reads:

> The return to Peace conditions has naturally ended the special training for women for Land Work which was undertaken at the College.

Farewell Rally of the Land Army

Drapers Hall, London
Nov. 27th, 1919, at 5.30 p.m.

PRESENTATION

OF THE

Distinguished Service Bars
of the Woman's Land Army

BY

Her Royal Highness PRINCESS MARY

SUPPER - - - - 7.15 p.m.

CONCERT - 8.30 p.m.

MORRIS DANCE	MIDDLESEX L.A.A.S.
SONGS ... { (a) "Coming thro' the Rye" } { (b) "Robin Adair" }	Miss JENNIE KIMMOND L.A.A.S.
VIOLIN SOLO	
SONG	Mr. FRANK CUTLER
DANCE WITH MOUTH-ORGAN } ACCOMPANIMENT }	{ Miss PAINTER } Cumberland { Miss SULLIVAN } { Miss FOSTER } L.A.A.S.
SONG	... Miss DONALDSON
DANCE ... ... "Spring Song"	Miss ENRIDGE, Worcs. L.A.A.S.
SONG	Miss DOROTHY WEBSTER
RECITATION ... ... { "The Song of England" } { (Alfred Noyes) }	Mrs. PETER GREGG
VENTRILOQUIST	
MORRIS DANCE	MIDDLESEX L.A.A.S.
SONG	... Miss DONALDSON
SONG	Mr. FRANK CUTLER
SONG	... Miss PAPWORTH
CLOG DANCE	Miss A. DENT
SONG	Miss KIMMOND

GOD SAVE THE KING

The Programme marking the Farewell Rally of the Women's Land Army.
Reproduced in *The Landswoman* in December 1919.

55

Miss Talbot wrote to the College:

> I am directed by the President of the Board of Agriculture and Fisheries to express his very warm appreciation of the good services which have been rendered by the Harper Adams Agricultural College to the Land Army in the matter of training recruits in agriculture, especially in tractor work. The subsequent success of the students is strong testimony to the excellent work which has been done at the College.

The American WLA

During the course of 1918 *The Landswoman* had reported the existence and activities of the American Women's Land Army. In 1917 a Standing Committee on Agriculture of the Mayor's Committee on Women on National Defence, in New York City, undertook to organise units of women farm workers. Each unit varied in number from six to seventy, the women living together in a centre from which they went out to work singly or in groups. The units were recruited very much along the lines of the National Land Service Corps, and were often college students or workers in various trades who wanted a change of occupation. These women borrowed a rallying cry from the women of the American Civil War:

Just take your gun and go,

For Ruth can drive the oxen, John,

And I can use the hoe.

Soon after America joined the Allies on the battlefields, the WLA of America was formed, taking advice from anyone who gave it, especially the Women's National Farm and Garden Union, which had already been responsible for a great interest in land work among American women. In February 1919 *The Landswoman* reported that an invitation had come from America for members of the British WLA to see their work at first hand. The invitation was never taken up, but arrangements *were* made for a Correspondence Club to operate between the two organisations. The idea was also floated for an exchange to take place; perhaps a scholarship for English women to attend agricultural colleges in America, and vice versa. During one of the big London rallies, in June 1919, the sight of sixty Land Army women leading 5,000 Home Service women on a march past Buckingham Palace impressed at least one American visitor, Miss Hamilton, head of the WLA of America. The event, organised by the War Savings Committee, was designed to draw public attention to the joys of saving their hard-earned pennies, as opposed to spending them. Whether or not it achieved its aim, Miss Hamilton said afterwards:

> I sail tomorrow, but before I go must tell you how proud I was of your Land Girls this afternoon. They looked so nice, so trim and capable, and I love that way they have of looking one straight in the eye. And may I say again how very, very much impressed I am by your whole organisation, and what you have accomplished. We have so much to learn from you, and I can hardly wait till I get back to tell our girls how much more capable yours are! But I

do hope that there will grow up a real sympathy and understanding between our two Land Armies, and that we may be just another link between our two nations.

Though few would argue with Miss Hamilton's assessment of the capability of the British Land Girls, it is to be hoped that her enthusiasm was not transmitted to her own women in quite those words. They might have taken a dim view of being thought second-best by the boss!

Demobilisation

The Women's Land Army was demobilised on 30 November 1919. Writing in *The Landswoman*, Lord Lee conveyed his official thanks:

> The war has furnished many inspiring examples of self-sacrifice and devotion to the country's cause, but none has been more conspicuous in that respect than the women who came to the help of the nation in its hour of need. Without the aid of women the manhood of the nation could not have withstood the attacks of our enemies, and the Women's Land Army is entitled to a specially honourable place among the various bodies into which women were organised. In spite of lower wages than might have been obtained in other occupations, and in spite of the isolation and discomforts of farm life, they came forward in large numbers to take the places of the men who had to leave the land for the Army.

He also recorded his admiration for the cheerfulness and spirit of comradeship which he thought had been conspicuous features of the WLA. He remarked on their pleasing uniform and their keen enthusiasm, which had done much to brighten the countryside. In the same, and last, official issue of *The Landswoman*, Meriel Talbot sent her own message, expressing thanks and sadness as the Land Army disbanded:

> While we are sad at the breakup of the Land Army we are grateful, deeply grateful, for the opportunity for service it has given us, for the manifold experience gained, and for the door opened to women to take their place in the agricultural life of the country.

One attempt to open that door had been made at the Edinburgh University Agricultural Society during the 1916-17 college year, when a Miss Bryden and a Miss Spiers had taken the floor at a Ladies' Night. Miss Bryden's paper was entitled 'The Part Played by Women in Agriculture during the War', and apparently was listened to with great attention, and acclaimed as one of the best heard for many years. Miss Spier's contribution, 'The Farmer's Wife as a Business Partner', was less well-received. The *Journal* of the Society records that she was 'too uncompromising, not to say radical, in her opinions as to the relative importance of husband and wife, to gain much support from her audience'!

The Staff at Swanley Horticultural College, July 1935.
From left to right.
Back row: Miss Ursula Newman; Miss Alcock; Miss Curling; Miss Batten; Miss Anderson;
Miss F.C. Schimmer; Miss Earles; Miss Huntbach.
Centre row: Miss Beatrice Oaks; Miss Wingell; Unidentified; Elizabeth Hess; W.E. Shewell-Cooper;
H. Smith; Miss Mary Page; Miss Campbell; Miss Given.
Front row: Miss FitzGerald; Miss Dickens; Miss Hilda C. Jameson; Dr. Kate Barratt; Miss Marian
Holmes; Mrs Craig; Mrs Stewart.

Swanley College continued in its determination to offer women the opportunity of a career on the land, although it meant a few changes for some of the ex-students. Princess Mary demonstrated her lasting interest by visiting the College in 1923. Swanley's historian, Elsa Morrow, recalls that, in 1921, the year before Dr Kate Barratt took over as Principal:

> The First Years, being untrained, did all the digging and heavy work, while the Second Years did the 'fancy' work in the greenhouses, taking cuttings, etc. Imagine our dismay when at the end of our First Year, it was decided that it was not right to expect girls straight from school and unused to hard physical work, to start digging and barrowing; in future the roles were reversed so we got let in for two years hard labour!

As a way of maintaining the spirit of comradeship, a new organisation - the National Association of Landswomen - was formed, in January 1920, to take the place of the WLA and Princess Mary was its Patron. With 'Unity is Strength' as its

58

slogan, the new Association sought a membership of at least 8,000. Both employers and the employed were invited to join, with the mutual object of maintaining and developing the status of women on the land.

Applicants were to be approved by the Local Committees in each county, and subscriptions were set at 4s. a year, or ld. a week. *The Landswoman* still functioned as 'The Journal of the Land Girl and Every Country Woman', and carried on much as before, although not for long. The spirit of comradeship now had no focus, and as women drifted back to their old lives, or became wives and mothers, the need for a new Association was wanting. Those able to take up the limited training opportunities offered did so, but, by July 1920, women still looking for a job on a farm were justified in giving up.

A scheme to merge the Landswomen's Association and the Women's Institutes, which shared similar interests and even membership, was presented to the Annual Meeting of the NFWI in 1922, but though it won the support of the NFWI Executive it was rejected by the Institute delegates. With amalgamation denied them, the Association found it impossible to continue an independent existence, and was disbanded.

The fortunes of the Women's Farm and Garden Union were as mixed, but at least it survived. In 1918 its membership stood at 1,100, and it had provided over 9,000 women with some kind of training. The ending of the war, however, meant that government grants were withdrawn, and, as women left the land, so membership declined. The chronic financial problems which had affected the Union from its inception in 1899 began again. The Union Clubhouse in Baker Street had proved of real benefit for members travelling through London, and in 1919 a move was made to larger premises in Park Street, which opened under the management of Miss Dunnell. In 1920, the 'Union' became 'Association', so as to avoid confusion over its role.

Mrs Roland Wilkins led a move in 1920 to buy a ninety-eight acre farm, and cottages, near Lingfield, in Surrey. This was divided up to form a smallholding colony for women who wanted to get a foot on the farming ladder. Not all tenants made a success of the chance offered to them, but many were able to relinquish their holdings after a few years, and move to larger farms, or buy their Lingfield smallholding - no mean achievement in the depressed agricultural conditions of the inter-war years. On an even more practical level, the WFGA's Council anticipated that once the Land Service Corps was disbanded it might be difficult for women land workers to buy suitable clothing. So, in 1921, an Outfit Department was started, buying shoes, overalls, and breeches wholesale, and storing them, to retail at a reasonable price to members. This service, as well as being used and appreciated by members, also made a modest profit for WFGA funds.

After moving to College Hall, Byng Place, in October 1931, the WFGA Council continued to work tirelessly to improve the training, salaries, and standing, of women seeking a career on the land. Byng Place, later renamed Courtauld House (after its benefactress Miss K. M. Courtauld), had previously been a Hall of

Residence for women students at London University, and was run exclusively by a small group of women, who, though most worthy in their ideals and devotion, were perhaps, by their age and class, ill-prepared for the immense social changes sweeping the country.

Agriculture between the Wars

The gradual improvements in farm prices, from 1930 onwards, were to come too late for many farmers whose debts had already forced them out of the industry. In March 1919, about half a million acres had come on to the market, and by 1920 land sales were even greater. In the years between the two wars arable land reverted to pasture at a fast pace, and by 1939 there were over a million fewer acres of arable land than in 1920. Farmers acknowledged that things would never be the same again. Research, accelerated by the war, was beginning to have its effect in all branches of farming. Speaking to the Plough Club at Oxford, in August 1922, Lord Ernle observed that 'the future of British agriculture is bound up in arable farming ... it is in the direction of tillage that science seems to be moving all along the line, and tillage could make the fullest use over the widest range, of scientific developments.'

Although thoughts of war were by then in the past, Lord Ernle might well have been remembering the prescient words of Lord Selborne, who, when trying to obtain long-term support for agriculture, in 1916, had said:

The dairy at Swanley, 1935.
Electricity was late in coming to the rural areas of northern Kent. Scenes like this were to continue for a further year.

Supposing twenty years hence our children have to face another such war, supposing the enemy we were fighting had built not fifty but five hundred first class submarines, and supposing that no answer to the submarine had been found in the meantime; where would be our food supply from overseas?

Agricultural research increased, and was encouraged in the years between the wars. It benefited from an £850,000 fund, granted by the Corn Production (Repeal) Act, 1921 - a further £500,000 being added in 1924 by Mr Noel Buxton, Minister of Agriculture. Other bodies, in universities and colleges, added to the flow of technical information. Regrettably, only the smallest proportion of this research and development filtered through to aid isolated family farms. The gap between the laboratory and the working farmer remained wide. The rural population benefited little from the new age of prosperity. Anyone out motoring during the 1920s and 1930s - an increasingly popular pastime for the wealthy - expected that once past the seemingly endless and badly planned estates of bungalows, villas, and council houses, romantic Britain would still be there: rustic, peaceful, and unhurried. A thatched cottage, with roses round the door, was the dream of many town dwellers; but if the roses were visible, they also camouflaged poverty and rural deprivation not far removed from that of the industrial slums. Many landed estates were maintained only by the income an owner obtained from outside farming. The Government had withdrawn price guarantees from farmers, and with them went the farm workers minimum wage. By 1928 home food production fell to a level at which sixty per cent of the total requirement was provided by imports. Unsurprisingly, men left the land in droves. In his *Scrapbook for the Twenties*, Leslie Baily writes:

In the fields men were erecting the pylons of the new electricity grid, but only four per cent of rural homes and farms had electricity. Few villages had piped water or main drainage; buckets were carried to pumps and springs, and the journey on a winter's night to the earth-closet at the bottom of the garden was one of the unsung experiences of country life.

During the 1920s women were breaking every tradition of dress and behaviour, though much less evidently in the country villages than in the towns. In 1928 the generation of 'flappers', women aged between twenty-one and thirty, were given the vote. In 1930 the licensing laws were altered so that unattended females were no longer excluded from entering public houses or restaurants at night. For women employed by the Civil Service, and in some other professions, progress was rather less perceptible. Although, in 1921, women civil servants were permitted to continue in their employment after marriage at the *discretion* of their employer, only eight married women were so-allowed in the years between 1934 and 1938. The rule was waived as a temporary expedient at the outbreak of the Second World War, but not finally abolished until 15 October 1946! New, and much-criticised, Family Planning Association clinics were set up by Dr Marie Stopes, who had fought a long battle in defence of a woman's right to limit the size of her family. Lady Denman was one of those who supported Dr Stopes and who upheld the new freedom offered by birth control. Active in the cause of rural women, Lady Denman, in 1918, was presiding over 760 Womens Institutes. By the beginning of 1928 there were 4,000 Institutes, and by 1939 they numbered well over 5,500 with a total membership of more than 350,000.

The Young Women's Christian Association (YWCA) also encouraged independence, while keeping an eye on morality. Its contribution to the Land Army during the war had been both practical and supportive. Instead of patriotic backslapping it had opened its Hostels to women land workers, even opening a convalescent home, in Margate, for weary Land Girls. In June 1919 the *Journal* of the YWCA expressed concern about the possible long-term effects of land work:

> A great many girls have renewed their health by land work, but some (and we must not forget them) have contracted serious permanent disabilities, such as rheumatism or glands. But all have made consistent sacrifices to 'carry on', and it is the due of all that their welfare should be studied until their services are no longer required.

The YWCA also had a Land Workers' Committee, opening the doors of its hostels in Bedford, Cambridge, Huntingdon, and Spalding. In Gloucester they had catered for forty forage girls. Concern for the women's spiritual welfare was expressed by invitations to Intercession services, and Land Girls could be certain of a welcome at any YWCA premises, especially after the Land Army disbanded.

The WIs, too, were growing in maturity, and began to involve themselves with other countrywomen across the world. A resolution adopted by the International Council of Women, meeting in Geneva in 1927, agreed to the formation of a committee 'to consider the conditions under which women's rural organisations worked.' Thus was born an international organisation representing over one hundred rural women's societies and institutes. By 1930, the ICW had agreed on the formation of a Liaison Committee of Rural Women's and Homemakers' Organisations. Finally, in 1933, came the creation of the Associated Countrywomen of the World (to which the Women's Farm and Garden Association was affiliated), with none other than Mrs Alfred Watt as its first President. A small committee represented the ACWW in London, and, in June 1939, with war looming, London hosted a meeting of the organisation. Twenty-three countries were represented, embracing a membership reaching from New Zealand, Ceylon, and Kenya, to Palestine, Latvia, and Romania. Germany was also represented. Cicely McCall, writing in *Women's Institutes*, told how the German woman's introduction caused a tense silence. An audience of nine thousand women held their breath to see what their reaction should be. Then came deafening applause:

> It fell, then grew again in increasing volume as though each perspiring delegate on that very hot June morning could not enough say: 'Welcome! We

are all countrywomen here to-day. We are non-party, non-sectarian. We wish for peace, goodwill and co-operation among nations. You have had the courage to come here in spite of rumours of wars. We bid you welcome!'

Much later, towards the end of the Second World War, Cicely McCall was to wonder what had happened to that German delegate, and indeed, whether she was still alive. One of the very first international moves by the National Federation of Women's Institutes after the war, was, in 1949, to host a tour for German women representatives of the Landfrauenvereine.

In the wake of the Great War it had been all too-easily assumed that conditions of life could only improve, and society continue to develop unhindered. The lessons had not been learned. When, in 1935, Walter Elliot, the Minister of Agriculture and Fisheries, set up a committee to consider food production in wartime the reaction of fellow cabinet members was not dissimilar to that which had greeted the Milner Committee's Report in 1915. Only with the heightened international tension in 1938 was the Cabinet prepared to discuss the question as one of national importance. It would appear that British governments can only think of home food production in times of crisis or shortage. Political neglect of agriculture was one of the main reasons why, by 1938, two million fewer acres were under cultivation than had been the case in 1914. Politicians were, of necessity, forced once again to turn their eyes towards the fields and meadows of rural Britain. This time there would be no hesitation. It was obvious where, and to whom, they would turn for labour in the coming crisis.

Lady Denman, with members of the administrative staff in the library at Balcombe Place.
Seated, to Lady Denman's right, is Mrs Margaret Pyke, Editor of The Land Girl.
Standing slightly behind Mrs Pyke, is Mrs Inez Jenkins, Deputy Director of the WLA.

5

Balcombe Place,
and the early years of the war

The Land Army fights in the fields. It is in the fields of Britain that the most critical battle of the present war may well be fought and won.

Lady Denman

The person best suited to taking on the task of setting up a new Women's Land Army was Lady Denman. She had experience of the recruiting drives of 1917-18, her name was synonymous with the Women's Institutes movement, and with rural affairs generally, and she had been Governor and Chairman of the Appeals Committee for Studley College.

At first, she was reluctant to take.on new responsibilities, since numerous other committees and projects already claimed much of her time. However, at the London Headquarters of the NFWI in Eccleston Street, top secret plans were finally made for a new Women's Land Army, with Lady Denman firmly at the helm. No doubt with memories of 1918 to the fore, she announced that the tasks of recruiting, assessing, placing, and catering for women farm workers must be done by a single body. She argued, too, that the women most suitable for county organising (though not for Land Army membership) should come from the WIs: raising the vexed question of where the non-affiliated, democratic, Institutes should stand in time of war.

Criticism had previously been aimed at the Institutes by Lord Lloyd, of the Navy League, who felt that the movement had infringed its rules by joining the League of Nations Union, the aim of which was to create an international union of women for peace. In the event of hostilities the WI would need to adhere to its principle of non-sectarianism, and, out of respect for its Quaker members, would have to impose some kind of restriction on the types of war work sanctioned by Headquarters. In the event, it was decided that the Institutes should be involved in assisting evacuees, or in similar schemes, but not in any air-raid precautions.

Later, when war service for women was made compulsory, some were persuaded to join the WLA rather than become conscientious objectors. Officially, there were 1,072 women conscientious objectors, of whom sixty-six were to be tried under the Defence of the Realm regulations, and imprisoned. Such women felt that the use of the word *army*, with its military overtones, was misleading - although in reality no woman joining the Women's Land Army was subject to military law. Afterwards, many perhaps echoed the words of one conscientious objector, who wrote, 'Unlike many others in the services we have happy memories to look back on. We didn't take life; we brought it into the world. I think our way of life benefited us more than it did those in the fighting.'

The final compromise on the use of the word 'army' in relation to land work, and the role of its members, caused little friction within the ranks of the WI or the WLA membership itself, although some were later to use it as a means of satirizing the Land Girl by suggesting that she was taking the 'soft option.' Women were to be depicted crazily at work in fields and meadows, hats askew, hair wind-blown and straw-covered. It was a bucolic image, unconsciously perpetrated by the women of the Land Army themselves. The Ministry of Information wished, in any case, to reassure the urban communities that the traditions of rural Britain were alive and kicking; what could be more appropriate than to bring before the public, merry, jubilant, harvesters skipping through primrose-studded rural byways? The fact that members of the easily identifiable WLA in no way represented the thousands of women and girls who normally worked the land was immaterial.

In May 1938, Lady Denman chose the heads of the county committees, and kept an eye on the activities of (amongst others!) the Dowager Lady Reading, who was at the same time putting her energies into setting up the Women's Voluntary Service (WVS). A certain amount of rivalry existed between those organisations poised to recruit female labour. Indeed, resentment was already evident amongst members of the Women's Farm and Garden Association, whose wartime support of the Land Army, and encouragement for women in agricultural and horticultural training and employment, had not ceased in 1919.

During the course of 1938, under the guidance of Miss Vanderpant, the Organising Secretary, the Association was sufficiently aware to set up a Land Service Scheme (LSS), successor to the 1914 Women's National Land Service Corps. It was assumed that the Land Service Scheme would operate in much the same way as the WNLSC had done, working alongside the WLA, and helping to maintain wartime food supplies.

By the close of 1938, there seemed little doubt in the minds of most people that war was inevitable, and Lady Denman was convinced of the need to have a force of willing women ready on day one. Having established the basis of an organisation she set about urging the Minister of Agriculture, the Rt. Hon. W. S. Morrison, to form the necessary committees. Then it was a question of keeping the momentum going, so that those women already pledged were not lost. In February 1939, she offered the Ministry of Agriculture the use of her own home, Balcombe Place, in which to house the headquarters of the new Women's Land Army, an offer not accepted by Mr Morrison's successor, Sir Reginald Dorman-Smith, until late July. In April she threatened to resign if she was not allowed to appoint her staff. This threat helped to concentrate minds wonderfully, and, on 1 June 1939, the new WLA was formed.

Lady Denman had first gone to Balcombe Place, at Haywards Heath in Sussex, in 1905, two years after her marriage to Lord Thomas Denman. The Victorian Tudor-style house, which had been bought by her father, was on a 3,000 acre estate, and included two other houses, one of which was let to Nellie Grant and her husband. The much-travelled Mrs Grant had accompanied Lady Denman on recruiting drives during the First World War. The WLA headquarters was established at Balcombe on 29 August 1939, five days before the declaration of war. Lady Denman was appointed its Honorary Director, and Mrs Inez Jenkins, Assistant Director. The Balcombe staff consisted of fourteen officers, and thirty-five clerks and typists, most living as well as working on the premises. The Chief Administrative Officer, and some of the typists, were from the Ministry of Agriculture in London, and their function was to maintain correspondence with other government departments and local authorities. A recruiting officer and two staff were also maintained in London, and it was this small office which received an unexpected visit, on the 1 September, from the Queen, who arrived looking pale and tired, but was 'graciousness itself' to the staff.

Balcombe Place was completely open to its new inhabitants. They were free to use the swimming pool or the music room, and could wander at will in the beautiful gardens - although the tennis courts were shared with a variety of livestock, including poultry, pigs, and rabbits. There were no rules, save that of strict punctuality at meal-times. Balcombe was, nevertheless, an awe-inspiring place for the WLA personnel, with its wide oak staircases, panelling, and red velvet curtains. The initial intake of staff had arrived at Balcombe station to be met by a fleet of chauffeur-driven cars, including a Rolls Royce! The WLA, like the earlier Women's Branch of the 1917 Food Production Department, was staffed and officered entirely by women. Seven of the senior members were Regional Officers, appointed to liaise with Headquarters, and to keep in contact with the fifty-three County Organisers, as well as helping to sort out any problems that might arise. Each officer was required to pay regular visits to the counties in her patch, and then to discuss national policy with her superiors and the other Regional members at periodic London meetings - some of which took place at Balcombe, in one of the many spare bedrooms which had been given over to offices. Each county appointed its own Organising Secretary, Chairman, committee, and sub-committees, as necessary. It was their job to interview and to place the volunteers, a task in which they received considerable help from the Village Representative. They also had a Salaries Secretary, who was responsible for welfare and conditions of employment.

From the beginning, it was made clear that the WLA was not intended for women already on the land. W. E. Shewell-Cooper, formerly Horticultural Super-

Office staff working at Balcombe Place.
'The splendid rooms are now filled with office-desks and trestle tables, piled with card-indexes and stationery, typewriters and telephones, pots of paste and Stickphast.'
(Vita Sackville-West)

intendent of the Swanley Horticultural College for Women, wrote in *Land Girl, A Manual for Volunteers in the WLA*:

> There always have been in peace-time thousands of women and girls working on the land, and it is not desired to recruit these into the Women's Land Army. They are asked to go on doing their important work; they are asked to remain in the villages where they live, and to work harder than ever ... the Women's Land Army is not for those who are already employed in agriculture, but for the volunteers who are willing to make agriculture their wartime profession.

In fact, there was more to it than merely an official 'desire' to recruit women from the towns. Professor D. R. Denman [no relation], who served on the War Agricultural Committee for Cumberland from 1941-5, wrote, in 'The Practical Application of Wartime Agricultural Policy':

Although not expressly provided as a condition precedent to enlistment the principle was established that no women who were experienced or employed in agriculture would be eligible to join the Land Army; the enrolment of female agricultural workers would have defeated the main object of the organisation - the provision of additional women as whole-time agricultural workers.

Those wives and daughters already on farms were not to expect a wage for doing what they did already, for which they seldom received much payment above the cost of their keep; and they could hardly expect to be allowed to join a Women's Land Army. No husband would have expected to pay his wife, and there were no 'State payments' to be had as the WLA itself never employed its members, performing only the function of an agency. It was the employer who was expected to shoulder the cost of employment. The War Agricultural Committees [or War Ags] were the largest employers of Land Girls, and each of these Committees organised gangs of women to work locally, paying them out of their own allocated funds. The point, as Professor Denman emphasised, was to *supplement* farm labour:

The volunteers were not employed by the Ministry or the directors of the organisation [WLA]. Their employment was contingent upon private contracts between the farmers or other employers (War Ags) and the volunteers themselves. Nevertheless, the Women's Land Army prescribed basic conditions of employment which both parties were required to accept - matters of living accommodation, wages, holidays, working hours, and other relevances - and supervised their implementation.

The clear distinctions made about the terms of employment were to prove of some consequence a few years later.

All those at Balcombe worked in close touch with the Ministry of Agriculture but were directly responsible, not only for general policy and administration, but also for successful negotiations when placing volunteers, and overseeing their wages and conditions. The county groups carried out government policies to the best of their capabilities, although this sometimes proved impractical. The Ministry considered that each county should aim to have a representative within bicycling or walking distance of every volunteer, and, if possible, farms were to be visited both before and after a member - whether in training or full employment - was placed. Where War Agricultural Committees acted as the direct employer for gangs the local representative was relieved of her duties. When it came to the jurisdiction of the Committees there was little that even a virtually autonomous WLA could do, other than relinquish control to the higher authority. Even the indomitable Honorary Director had to give way to the vagaries of the War Ags. She did not, however, see any reason why she should do the same for the Women's Farm and Garden Association. The differences of opinion which arose between the WFGA Council and Lady Denman in 1939 were to leave her with many lifelong critics. The inevitable, and admitted, élitist attitude among women trained for farm work, saw an undermining in the WLA of the fragile status which had been fought for so hard. The 1940 Annual Report made it clear that the Women's Farm and Garden Association was committed to safeguarding the position of trained and experienced women when they might be 'seriously affected by an influx of temporary volunteers'. Although Lady Denman was a member of the WFGA, the Association was offered no corporate part in the Land Army enterprise. Undeterred, the Association's Land Service Scheme set out instead to give inexperienced women the opportunity to acquire some practical skills, and to provide others with farm experience during their holidays, or at weekends. Such a task, the WFGA Council reasoned, would be their independent and supporting wartime role; but even this was denied to them. Lady Denman was determined that the task of supplying female labour to farms should be done by one single organisation - her own! Training was also to come under her jurisdiction. Semi-trained WFGA women were ineligible for enlistment, neither could they be re-employed as trained. The official History of the WFGA laments:

> This was very unfortunate, as a number of mistakes and defects in the organisation of the Land Army during the Second World War could have been avoided if people with real practical experience had been involved beforehand. Of equal importance to the Association, an opportunity was missed of offering Courtauld House to the authorities as a WLA hostel or clubhouse for the duration.

Courtauld House remained open, following the outbreak of war, until it suffered severe bomb damage in September 1940, and was evacuated. The Association did not regain possession until 1945. During the war years the WFGA, the feathers of its matriarchs ruffled, played a low-key role in women's land work. Occasional meetings were held under the chairmanship of Dr Kate Barratt, the Principal of Swanley College, and it had to content itself with memorandums, publications concerning the conditions of work and pay for women, the Garden Apprenticeship Scheme, and contributing when and where it could to Ministry committees. Though demoted in organisational importance, the Association nevertheless did much, both during and after the war, to improve the lot of those women outside the protection of the Land Army. With its emphasis on the importance of training and professionalism, the Association managed to retain its integrity - it had after all been in existence since before the turn of the century - and it was to have a peacetime role denied to Lady Denman's volunteer army.

Undeterred by the WFGA hiccup, Lady Denman's single-minded efficiency paid off in terms of enrolment. At the end of December 1939, the WLA numbered 4,544 members, and by April 1940, nearly 6,000 of the enrolled 11,000-12,000 recruits were in agricultural employment. Others were temporarily unavailable or free for part-time or local work only. Some enrolled as non-mobile members, continuing to live and work on their family's farm - although this came to an abrupt end once the policy of enlisting only untrained women was established. Credit for the constructive and systematic planning that managed to get so many women motivated and on to the farms has to be attributed to Lady Denman herself: her personal strength of character steamrolling aside any opposition or suggestion of failure. She was a force for efficiency, passionately dedicated to her belief in the individual woman, and resolute in her defence of democracy. She had led the Women's Institutes along just such a path, resulting in undreamt of improvements in the lives of ordinary country women.

She was determined that such bureaucracy as needed to exist, would also make life at least tolerable for the Land Girls. If the relationship between the Honorary Director and officialdom was never particularly easy one incident, occurring early in the War, empasised that Lady Denman was a force to be reckoned with. During November 1939, the suggestion was made, within the Ministry of Agriculture, that 'inasmuch as the Honorary Director is a woman, such an attention from the Minister, although unprecedented, might not be inappropriate.' The 'attention' involved the sending of a personal Valentine greeting from Sir Reginald Dorman-Smith, the Minister, to Lady Denman, to be made the following February. In a tantalisingly incomplete memo, dated 24 November 1939, an official opined that:

> In view [of the] probable course of events, I consider that the suggested action by the Minister may tend to ease a situation which will almost certainly have become tense by February 14th.

It will forever be uncertain whether the *situation*, whatever it may have been, was eased by a Valentine that took four months to organise, and involved over twenty inter-departmental memos. It required too, not only the co-operation of the Treasury, but also that department's sanction on costs: which included an estimate from Messrs Allover, Allover and Allover, for red fabric hearts at a cost of a penny three farthings each! The Treasury expressed doubts that any useful purpose would be served by the proposal, but, 'as the Minister of Agriculture approves the scheme, the Treasury will raise no insuperable objection.' Further estimates for material were obtained; there was considerable discussion about possible colours for lettering and decoration, in view of War shortages; and the Minister announced that he did not like the draft wording. In view of the fact that a war was taking place, it is highly improbable that the Valentine (duly delivered in 1940) - 'Tape is Red and Pencils Blue, Sugar is Beet and So are You! - did other than convince the unsentimental Lady Denman that bureaucracy had indeed gone mad!

Having experienced one World War and its aftermath, she was well able to guage the changes that had occurred in society's attitude to women, and the demands being placed upon them. She anticipated that while the women of the Land Army during the First World War had had to put up with a great deal of public (predominantly male) chaffing and vilification, the new generation of Land Girls would have to face different problems.

For many girls the WLA represented their first taste of personal freedom; and if the notion of innocents being sent to isolated farms was bad enough, the alternative - a Hostel in the middle of the countryside - was not necessarily guaranteed to improve morality. Indeed, according to John Costello, author of *Love, Sex and War*, the coming of the American GIs to Britain put many a Land Girl in moral jeopardy:

> For all their generosity, the GIs soon acquired a reputation for resorting to a frontal assault when it came to getting the 'cute piece of ass' they were always chasing. It was not unusual for 'Snowdrops', as the US military police were known from their distinctive white helmets, to be summoned to lift a siege at rural hostels which housed Land Girls.

No wonder Lady Denman was concerned, or that the YWCA opened wide its doors! The Association, indeed, was eventually to manage one hundred and forty-six hostels on behalf of the WLA, endeavouring to make the volunteers 'healthy and happy, and at the same time, give them educational and recreative facilities'. There was no way round the hostels argument. If the girls were not housed in groups how else were they to form travelling gangs, the need for which had been demonstrated by the women of the 1914-18 war.

Co-ordinating supply and demand remained a perpetual hurdle in the way of true agricultural efficiency. So often, in the First World War, women had been in the right place but at the wrong time, and at the start of the Second World War it looked like happening again. To meet the short-term problems, an Auxiliary Force was set up at the request of the Minister of Agriculture. In May 1940, a message went out via the pages of the WI journal, *Home and Country*:

> Recruits are wanted now for this new force. They are asked to enrol for at least a month or for longer if they can. Those recruits who are 18 years or over will get a minimum wage of 28s. a week. Many of them will work in groups, they may camp out in tents or in empty houses or they may be billeted with local families. They will have to pay for their board from the wages they receive.

The Auxiliary Force caused some confusion on paper as it distorted the official figures and made assessment of WLA membership impossible at times. By September 1942, when the official WLA strength had increased to 52,000, some of that number was certainly accounted for by the Auxiliary Force. It was not to be a prolonged success in England and Wales, but it became better-established in Scotland.

Since the War Ags were responsible for large numbers of Land Girls, it was they who negotiated billets for workers where accommodation could not be provided by the farmers. Where this demand was acute, and where negotiations for voluntary co-operation failed, the Minister of Health, through the local authorities, exercised his powers under the Defence Regulations. Professor Denman recalls that residential hostels were provided 'either in new buildings erected for the purpose by the Ministry of Works, or in requisitioned premises', and that one such, Aspatria Hall in Cumberland, was a total failure. This was due not to any administrative bungling but to the fact that, after their very first night of occupation, the Land Girls refused to remain there. Aspatria Hall, they announced with one voice, 'was haunted'! Despite an invasion of exorcists from London ('the whole room became frozen like a morgue, and a ghastly smell pervaded') the Land Army never returned. They might be prepared to fight the rigours of farm life, but ghosts, never!

In 1941, when women became liable for conscription under the National Service Act, protection was given to female workers in agriculture, agricultural engineering, gardening (provided eighty per cent of the time was concerned with the production of vegetables), and to women who had been in such employment prior to the registration. This latter protection applied, naturally enough, to members of the Women's Land Army. However, in 1942, a directive to the Ministry of Labour to increase the flow of women on to the land caused considerable friction. The old enemy, dual control of labour, was once again to result in an overlapping of recruitment, and much confusion. In August 1943, it was estimated that 87,000 women were in some way connected with actual food production, but the accuracy of the figures left much to be desired. Although the number represented a wartime record it coincided with an acute shortage of labour in the aircraft industry. Recruitment for the land was then slowed down, and women directed instead into aviation. For both the individual farmer and the Land Girl, the compilation of statistics was irrelevant. Indeed, on occasions, it re-enforced a belief that officials spent a large part of their days chasing their own tails. It is a mistaken belief that in an emergency bunglers do anything more than bungle. Farmers were constantly being monitored, and a steady stream of officials was entitled to come on to their farms telling them what to grow, whom to employ, and how much they should pay.

Land Girls found, however, to their amusement, that where one avenue of recruitment was closed another would eventually open. Many girls turned down by one of the recruiting agencies had only to contact another to receive a more positive response.

In Scotland, recruitment was run by the Department of Agriculture for Scotland, and its WLA operated much along the lines as that of Balcombe although the members faced a great deal more opposition from Scottish farmers. In November 1943, the total strength of the Scottish WLA reached 7,967 - the greatest number being in Ayr (1,160), Fife and Kinross (664).

The WLA was also represented in the Isle of Man, and in Northern Ireland. The Isle of Man Land Army was a mobile force, with its base at the Government's experimental farm, near Peel, where training was given. Mobile Squads were formed, and operated out of Peel. They travelled in their own vans, in gangs ranging from two to ten girls, according to the particular seasonal needs. Women here received the same uniform as those on the mainland, but their wages were lower: £2 4s. 6d. per week. They also worked longer hours: sixty hours a week - with only one half day, and one Sunday free per fortnight.

In the case of Northern Ireland the situation is difficult to assess statistically, as compulsory National Service was never introduced and, consequently, recruitment was lower. Despite its shipyards and heavy industry, it was a country still largely tied to a rural economy, where many eligible women were already involved in agriculture; those who were not often found the option of a town job more attractive, particularly daughters anxious to escape from their home environment.

Even the Scilly Isles had a tiny WLA contingent. Land Girls worked on at least three of the five inhabited islands, including Tresco (only three miles by one - with its harbour, church, single shop, and post office), whose long and narrow fields of vegetables were cultivated for export. Although frosts are rare, the winds sweep across the Isles with hurricane force, so that tall windbreaks of shrubs or rush matting are needed to shield the crops. Here, early potatoes, tomatoes, onions, and cabbages were grown by an isolated band of WLA members.

Who then were the women who volunteered for active farm service at the outbreak of war, and who were to find their first taste of farm life coinciding with the worst winter on record? The *Journal* of the Ministry of Agriculture described them as 'workers from shops and offices, mannequins, actresses, domestic servants, and typists', to name but a few. It was estimated that one third of Land Army recruits came from London and Middlesex, or the industrial areas of both Lancashire and Yorkshire. A few were from overseas, either naturalized Britons or friendly aliens exiled by the war. Although the official age for enlistment was eighteen the Land Army did not require birth certificates, so many volunteers were able to substitute the minimum enlistment age for the correct one! If there were those who still looked upon the countryside as a romantic escape from a sheltered home life, many more sought adventure, while still others were simply seeking employment wherever they could find it. Although recruitment for the WLA was a high priority, jobs were not always immediately forthcoming. One administrator at the WLA recruiting office, at the beginning of September 1939, wrote:

> The spirit of co-operation and comradeship at the office is wonderful but I am sorry for so many poor youngsters who come up for land work. They have lost their jobs and are desperately in need of employment. They throw themselves completely on one's mercy but they must wait. There are so many hundreds that must be placed before the newcomers.

Farmers were not, it seemed, taking on untrained women, and this, combined with an inflexible recruitment campaign, meant that things moved slowly. In retrospect, the lack of urgency during the 'Phoney War' was understandable. Later on, when the standards of recruitment were further blurred and the national need even greater, there was more certainty of employment; but by then munitions and factory work were exerting a greater pull on a recruit's attention. For those outside the industrial centres the Land Army represented a kind of Hobson's Choice. Many were forced to take what they could get, including those women obliged to register for National Service in 1940, and those in 1941, when all unmarried and childless women between nineteen and thirty years of age became liable for war service. In 1943 the age for registration was raised to fifty-one, and many who chose farm work had to put up with taunts of 'soft option' - the public still being largely ignorant of the nature of farm work. In cases where a woman found herself being taken advantage of by an unscrupulous employer, using WLA members for work unconnected with agriculture, she would usually leave of her own volition. Only rarely did incidents come to light where a Land Army job had been *fixed* so that a woman need neither leave home nor join the Services. Not all motives for joining were ideal, but one, unashamedly at least, put on record her own reasons. In 1945, a writer in the *Eastern Daily Press* commented in 'A Land Girl Looks Back':

Although I have always lived in the country, until I worked on the land I used to rather scorn farmers and farming, and jeer at my family who were always talking about it; thinking it a very dull and boring subject. Then the war came, and as I was very anxious to stay at home and not be sent into the Forces, land work seemed the only possible thing.

Perhaps she was one of the many who responded to the recruiting talks given by Lady Denman on the BBC. Certainly Lady Denman could make a favourable contrast between the modern microphone as an aid to communication, and that of the First World War, when she and Nellie Grant had proclaimed the Land Army's recruiting message. As the result of one such broadcast, on 15 January 1941, Balcombe Place was able to announce that over one thousand applications had been received. In addition to Lady Denman's radio broadcasts there were numerous talks on food production and country matters, on subjects ranging from 'Feeding the Land' and 'Our Changing Countryside', to 'The Changing Shape of the Village' and 'Rural Buildings, Old and New.' Donald McCullough, famous as Chairman of the BBC's Brains Trust, was involved in several programmes highlighting the role of the WLA. One of these took place on 20 May 1943, when the attention of listeners was drawn to the part played by overseas members of the WLA. This 'Empire Discussion' programme was really a Ministry of Information Press Conference, and Miss Joan West, a Canadian participant, recalled the occasion:

Four more Land Girls arrived, one from Malta, one from Rhodesia, one from Australia; and there was a Dutch girl from British Guiana. We were taken to a large hall and seated. There Mr McCullough introduced us to the overseas reporters. Miss Brew, who handles the LA publicity, made a speech about the work of the LA, and then the reporters were turned loose on us. I had three to cope with.

75

Fortunately all three questioners were kind, one even offering to help Miss West travel to Europe after the war! After the initial briefing, they did a five minute recording sitting round a small table and speaking into 'a wire ball suspended above the table'. The party later visited the WLA recruiting office in Oxford Street:

It has an attractively decorated window with photographs of Land Girls at their work. Our real destination, however, was the Land Army Park Lane attachment, and here we were photographed bending over broad beans and trying to look knowledgeable. As we had been photographed previously at the Ministry of Information, I, for one, was getting tired of photographers.

Tea was taken at Stewarts in Oxford Street (this being the first meal of the day for Miss West) after which they were free for the rest of the afternoon. That evening, she returned to her job in Abbots Ripton, reassured that her contribution to Miss Brew's publicity venture would be broadcast to the Empire!

After the war had ended, WLA members were still invited to participate in BBC broadcasts, but, by 1948, it was to take part in television programmes like 'Picture Page'.

The winter of 1939-40 was the harshest in living memory, and the glittering array of shop assistants and secretaries were given the ultimate test of endurance and fortitude. They played a leading role in making ready over two million new arable acres for the spring planting. Some assistance may be said to have come from the growth in mechanisation, though doubtless better and more practical clothing, together with improved footwear, contributed immeasurably. The acceptance of a woman's need to wear breeches, and other articles of clothing which would help free and efficient body movement, was one major difference between the position of women in 1939 and those of the 1915 generation.

The official uniform, issued to every WLA member, consisted of:

Two green jerseys	One pair of gumboots, or boots with leggings
Two pairs breeches	One hat
Two overall coats	One overcoat with shoulder titles
Two pairs of dungarees	One oilskin or mackintosh
Six pairs of stockings	Two towels
Three shirts	One oilskin sou'wester
One pair of ankle boots	A green armlet and a metal badge
One pair of shoes	

For every six months good service, members could add a half-diamond badge to the armlet - diamonds were given for twelve months service - with a special armlet to be awarded after two years continuous and satisfactory service. After four years service this was replaced by a scarlet one. Good service badges were highly prized, and these membership barometers were well-publicised in *The Land Girl* and the local county news sheets. Although the uniform was described as 'free', the member had to surrender the required number of clothing coupons, and a replacement was only allowed after twelve months. The combination of a green jersey and brown hat, offically described as, 'practical, not unattractive', was greeted by many with less than enthusiasm. 'Not unattractive' presumably, in this case, meant totally unbecoming!

Shortly after Robert (later first Viscount) Hudson was appointed Minister of Agriculture in 1940, Lady Denman complained that the Ministry was not taking the WLA seriously enough. The girls suffered from being thought rather comical, were a butt for Press caricatures, and much of it had to do with how the uniform was worn. This question was not so hotly discussed as it had been in 1916, but when the matter arose it had usually to do with hats. Indeed the wearing of the WLA hat was to prove something of a battle between officialdom and the membership. It was not so much what was worn, as *how* it was worn. Members of the Women's Voluntary Service were encouraged to wear their hats in individual styles, but Land Army girls were supposed to wear theirs at a uniformly straight angle over reasonably controlled hair. In his *Land Girl, A Manual for Volunteers in the Women's Land Army*, W. E. Shewell-Cooper made the official position quite clear: 'Volunteers are asked to wear their hat correctly, and are reminded that a good volunteer is a good advertisement.'

As Vita Sackville-West was to put it in the 1944 Ministry of Agriculture handbook, *The Women's Land Army*:

> She could look as romantic as a cowboy in it if she liked; and indeed, on a reduced scale, it is not unlike the hats affected by the once popular Tom Mix and his colleagues ... the original intention of the Ministry of Agriculture was to provide her with a hat designed for the work she had to do, supplying a shady brim over the eyes and a protection for the back of the neck. The result is neither one thing nor the other. It is neither useful, romantic, nor smart in either the uniform or the fashionable sense. It is merely comic, as comic as a music-hall turn.

Vita Sackville-West also wondered whether any of them ever looked in a mirror, and added:

> She builds her hair up in such a way that no hat could possibly be expected to remain in place, adds a bootlace to her hat, and uses it as a chin strap, trying, presumably, to make an ornament out of it, not realising that to the casual observer she looks as though she were suffering either from toothache or from mumps ... She seldom wears her hat at all when working ... she doesn't prefer to go bareheaded, she usually ties her head up in a coloured scarf, a practice which I find pretty, practical, peasant-like and consequently pleasing.

A full page of 'The Land Army Hat and How to Wear it', appeared in *The Land Girl* during August 1940, replete with photographs, to persuade members to wear their hats correctly, although it is unlikely that anyone took much notice of such pedantic instructions.

In her book, *If Their Mothers Only Knew*, Shirley Joseph observes that Land Girls quickly learned that it was a point of honour always to look as dirty and unkempt as possible, just to show how hard they worked! Numerous complaints concerning the wearing of the uniform continued to filter through to Balcombe, although it is not always easy to assess quite who was making them. Vita Sackville-West cites one instance in which a complaint of untidiness was made by an ATS girl. No member of the ATS, of course, had to spend hours in muddy fields, often in driving rain, and then be asked to muck out the cow sheds or piggeries, either in or out of uniform. Neither was the ATS necessarily faced with turning out in an 'average-sized' uniform.

Orders for WLA uniforms were referred to the Ministry of Supply, whose Materials Committee would be consulted as to availability. Most of the uniforms spent some part of their life stored in the squash courts or stables at Balcombe Place. Lady Denman in particular took a rather eccentric interest in the length of the overcoat. If women had found the length of the coats during the First World War frustrating, the new Honorary Director now considered the modern coats too short. Her own tailor altered the design, and lengthened the coats, albeit after a considerable battle for an extra material allowance. Delays of six months between orders and delivery were not unusual, and often resulted in a girl turning out in a uniform of mixed sizes. More than one recruit remembers the hilarity that ensued when she first put on the uniform, which had probably been ordered by post. Nothing fitted - but, after all, there was a war on!

6
Land Girl and Country Woman

On September 11 my employer led me, with what I now know to be mutual doubts, out to his orchards to start picking plums, and there he left me, with a completely uncontrollable ladder, two picking baskets and a pile of empty half-sieves. I had no idea of the lay-out of the farm, and when he disappeared into the blue, to do I knew not what, with an unknown possible team of workers, I felt more alone, lost, desolate and incompetent than ever in my life before. Apart from anything else, I have a horror of heights in general, and ladder-heights in particular!

E. M. Barraud, (No. 9600), The Land Girl, 1940.

It had been accepted from the outset that the Second World War would require the mobilisation of the entire adult population. For the WLA the issue remained that of persuading women to assist in maintaining food supplies, and in preventing those women already at such work from leaving. For those in charge of recruitment at Balcombe Place the problem was to play down the likelihood of isolation. Except for those billeted in hostels, or mobilised into gangs, the membership had no real community existence. The majority of new landworkers were to be employed by individual farmers or estates, and many of these women were suddenly to be brought face to face with the harsh realities of country living, as well as with the problems brought about by loneliness or an understandable homesickness. In addition to draughty farmhouses, and possible exploitation, there were less predictable problems. During 1940, many County Organisers were to receive complaints from Land Girls about the difficulties of finding their way around, and not just in the blackout; even in broad daylight the task was complicated by the enforced removal of those deceptively simple aids to rural life - signposts!

The success of *The Landswoman* in strengthening morale during the First World War encouraged the WLA to organise a similar publication for its members. Launched on 1 April 1940, and priced at 3d., *The Land Girl* was to play an inestimable role in disseminating information - sweetening it where necessary - and keeping the WLA together, in spirit at least. Caught between being thought of as 'ignorant townies' by the rural population, or eccentrics 'gone-native' by fellow urbanites, WLA members needed all the morale boosting they could get, and this came firmly in the guise of hearty encouragement from the Editorial office. While *The Land Girl* did tackle political or controversial issues where they affected its readers, the war naturally imposed restrictions on content. Throughout its life, the magazine was to be edited by Mrs Margaret Pyke who, when war was declared, was already living at Balcombe. Mrs Pyke had met and shared Lady Denman's enthusiasm for the WI movement during the 1930s, as well as having responsibilities on Family Planning committees in common. Under her editorship *The Land Girl* eventually attained a circulation of 21,000 copies a week. As the Editor noted in the first issue:

> There is a curious delusion that land workers are rather slower than town folk; that, like brains and brawn, cows and culture don't go together. Perhaps it all depends on what is meant by culture. There is certainly more cash and more comfort attached to the commercial or clerical city existence. Whether it also shows a better sense of values or proves the possession of superior brains is quite another matter.

To begin with, *The Land Girl* was an unofficial publication, but, by 1942, it was seen to be so influential that the Ministry of Agriculture agreed to fund it. Each issue was filled with readers' contributions, hints, guides for work in the fields, news, and reviews on related subjects. Lady Denman particularly enjoyed the humorous touches which the magazine included - such as the would-be recruit who wrote that she wanted to learn to milk, but would like to begin on a calf; or the letter from a girl who had been unable to attend church because she had ploughed in her Land Army hat! In January 1941, Mrs Pyke welcomed in the New Year, telling her readers that things were looking (prematurely as it turned out) a good deal more cheerful than they had a few months earlier. The liveliest optimist would not have imagined, 'that before the year was out we should have taken the offensive in the Near East . . . defeated Mussolini's long-prepared threat to Egypt and invaded Italian territory.' On the subject of food production, however, it was business as usual:

> For the Women's Land Army, 1941 looks like being a big year. It is obvious that the food problem is one of the hardest we have to solve, and our Minister has said that he will want 40,000 of us to help him solve it. Recruiting will be in full swing shortly, and when the new recruits come along the old hands will have a big part to play.

It was indeed to be a significant year for home agriculture. Food imports (including fifty per cent of domestic meat consumption) had hardly been affected during the period of the 'phoney war'. However, the Ministry of Food (set up in 1939), had to

THE LAND GIRL

No. 12. Vol. I.   MARCH 1941   Price 3d.

A PRIZE—
AND A QUESTION

"**P**LEASE forgive me for bothering you, but I am quite distracted about my garden, and think that perhaps you could help me," wrote a would-be employer of the Land Army to Lady Denman a few days ago. Just now there are many farmers and horticulturists who are distracted about their cows or their crops, their trees and their vegetables, and who are turning to us for help. The Land Army is giving that help as fast as it can, but it is entirely dependent on two things—on getting new members and on keeping old ones.

As a contribution to the first problem THE LAND GIRL offers a prize of two guineas to the member of the Land Army who produces the greatest number of new volunteers by May 25th, 1941. She must prove to the satisfaction of her County Secretary that it was her suggestion or persuasions which induced the new volunteers to join, and only those who have been interviewed, enrolled and accepted for training will count.

As to the second problem, the wastage rate of the Land Army is not high, but it could certainly be lower than it is. The Navy, Army and Air Force fight the battles of the nation, but it is the workers of the land who have got to feed the nation, and deserters are a liability we cannot afford. Sometimes the choice whether to go or stay is not easy, and your reasons for wishing to leave the Land Army may seem very strong. In that case, try asking yourself this question : "Suppose I can't be replaced? Suppose in the coming hard months a child goes hungry because I left my job? Shall I feel then that I was justified in doing so?" If you can answer "yes" to that question, then go with a clear conscience. If not, stay, and be proud of staying.

M. A. P.

The front cover of *The Land Girl*, March 1941.
The magazine was designed to boost the morale of its scattered readership.

81

acknowledge, by the end of 1940, that shipping losses had dramatically increased, and that the situation - for a nation relying for practically all of its requirements of sugar, flour, fats and cereals on imports - was critical. Government estimates for imports had to be reduced by five million tons during the first three months of 1941 after Germany had intensified its attacks on merchant shipping. Even the foodstuffs sent under the American 'Lease-Lend' scheme were insufficient to prevent the implementation of stricter rationing.

The Land Girl was one of several women's magazines which continued to be published throughout the war, but although it had much in common with the likes of *Woman*, or *Woman's Own*, it was aimed at a specialist audience. It was in fact more like a club magazine, and so unlikely to find a large readership outside the WLA membership. The reference to 'girl' in the title was significant. Women on the land during the Great War had been thought of, and treated as, women. The harum-scarum Green Jerseys of the 1940s presented a much more girlish, swashbuckling image. For advertisers, *The Land Girl* provided a clear target; although it is strange that while the Tampax message, 'No "off days" now', and accompanying analgesics, appeared in most of the wartime magazines for women, none appeared in *The Land Girl*. While the readers of popular magazines might look forward to 'Beauty in a few Minutes from Icilma Beauty Aids', 'Tangee Lipstick for Beauty on Duty', and 'Aertex Corsets', Land Girls were urged to 'Look Smart in Hebden Breeches', 'Make the Job go with a Swing: Made to Measure Jodhpurs', and 'Felt Flowers are Fun to Make'!

A deliberate attempt was made to encourage those from a town background to blend into their new environment. In his WLA Manual, *Land Girl*, W. E. Shewell-Cooper writes:

> Town girls on the whole use far more make-up than country girls. The Women's Land Army volunteer should therefore be prepared to 'tone down' her lips, complexions and nails considerably. A certain amount of make-up may be used at parties and local village dances, but long nails are quite unsuited to work on a farm, especially when covered with bright crimson nail-varnish. The volunteer will soon find that, as the other girls from the village do not use make-up, she will prefer not to use it herself, so as not to look conspicuous. She will find, too, that she will get such a healthy colour to her cheeks that rouging will not be necessary!

While *The Land Girl* was circulating its message to WLA volunteers, the WIs journal, *Home and Country*, taking its name from the motto of the movement, was similarly employed in keeping rural spirits high when necessary. Started in 1919 by Alice Williams, a Welsh bard, and briefly Honorary Secretary of the National Federation, the editorship was taken over, two years later, by Mrs Nugent Harris, an energetic no-nonsense Adviser to the training schools for Voluntary County Organisers.

Although there is little overlapping news or information about the WLA in *Home and Country* during the war years, as the WI membership was a separate body with its own identity, the activities of the WLA were occasionally mentioned, as, for example, in June 1940, when *Home and Country* readers were told about the publication of *The Land Girl* magazine:

> The first number contains an inspiring message from Lady Denman ... and some very sensible first aid advice for land workers that would be useful to every country dweller.

Though Land Army members were rarely allowed a platform, one WLA member, Miss Gould, was able to write to the journal, in March 1941, to say how much she and her colleagues had appreciated the kindness shown to them by local WI members:

> In some instances girls have found the land work even harder than they had expected, and aching muscles and intense loneliness had made them ready to resign. Often they have not done so because they suddenly found some friendly souls who have invited them in to a cup of tea or cocoa, and an evening chat or game, or offered them hot baths. My friend and I have been working in the Land Army since the outbreak of war and have had varied experiences. In one village, although almost everything else was arranged for our comfort, hot baths were considered a luxury! People had not realised what a necessity they were to WLA workers, especially to beginners. Therefore if you have the facilities for offering hot baths, please remember the Land Army.

Always anxious to convey news of the lives of women from overseas, *Home and Country* nurtured the special links which their countrywomen had with Canada and the United States of America. Its pages reflect the increasing internationalism that war, and the mutual sympathies of those affected by war, had generated. The visit to North America by Miss Janet Strang, Chief Instructress at the Northamptonshire Institute of Agriculture, was widely reported, not only in *Home & Country* and *The Land Girl*, but in other contemporary journals and farming magazines. Miss Strang was one of four agriculturalists invited to take part in a lecture tour by the United States Department of Agriculture, which did much to promote good relations between the two countries. Countrywomen across the world were making a major contribution towards understanding and co-operation, as *Home and Country* was able to report in January 1945:

> Two hundred Countrywomen's Associations in Queensland, Australia, have each linked up with an English WI and are exchanging regular correspondence. In December last came the welcome news that 200 cakes

were on their way to this country for the Christmas tea-tables, rich fruit cakes of a type that most WI members have not seen for six years. The generosity of Dominion countrywomen is a continual joy and wonder to us over here. WIs in Alberta, Canada, have sent £242 for the relief of bomb distress, and this may well make the phrase 'A Happy New Year' true for more than one bombed-out family.

In addition to the WLA's national magazine, several counties started their own news-sheets, usually distributed inside copies of *The Land Girl*. One of these, the *Kent News Sheet* announced its first (undated) issue thus:

> Kent is to have its own News Sheet. It will include items of special interest to the County, but not general WLA information which can be found in *The Land Girl*. It is very much to be hoped that WLA workers themselves will contribute. Our space is necessarily limited, but any letters containing stories of experiences on the farms, jokes, suggestions, and comments will be carefully considered for publication if sent to the News Sheet Editor.

The Editor of the news-sheet was no less than Vita Sackville-West, although her youngest son, Nigel Nicolson, questions whether she personally edited it as she was 'already well-occupied'. However she received the credit, and undoubtedly inspired it. Certainly there would have been no lack of editorial material, with Swanley College so near, and solid back-up provided by Lady Cecily Cornwallis, Chairman of the Kent WLA, Miss V. M. M. Cox, Organising Secretary, and Mrs Heron Maxwell, all of whom were keen to publicise WLA activities.

Vita Sackville-West's association with the WLA started at the very beginning of the war - she had her first meeting with the Maidstone Committee on 14 September 1939, and was not to relinquish her responsibilities until June 1945. She, with her husband Harold Nicolson, and their two sons, had moved to Sissinghurst Castle in 1930. Her WLA role was that of District Representative for an area stretching from Tenterden, in the central Weald, to Lamberhurst. Once a fortnight, throughout the war, she visited farms, enrolled suitable recruits, called on the club that she helped to found in Sissinghurst village hall, and attended Maidstone Committee meetings, as well as presiding over fund-raising fetes.

The Honourable Victoria Mary Sackville-West - called Vita so as to distinguish her from her similarly titled mother - was born in 1892, and was eight years Gertrude Denman's junior. The two women, whose names are linked indelibly with the history of the WLA, expressed their intellectual and practical independence in very different ways. As a woman, Vita was prevented from inheriting Knole House in Kent, her birthplace and ancestral home. She was an impecunious aristocrat with a fascination for 'the rich'. Lady Denman, on the other hand, enjoyed the rewards of her father's prosperity; her husband, Baron Denman, had inherited his title from an impoverished great uncle. Their

Vita Sackville-West at Sissinghurst, c. 1944.

differing perceptions are apparent in the letter Vita wrote to her eldest son in 1943, describing a visit to Balcombe Place to discuss the writing of the WLA Handbook:

I had Lord Denman's bedroom (minus Lord D) and amused myself very much by opening all the large cupboards and admiring his array of suits, hats, shoes and hunting-crops. So that is how the rich live! A glass of milk, two biscuits, and a jug of orangeade were put out on what is politely called the night-table beside my bed, and there was a lovely writing table with stacks of note-paper and new Relief nibs in the pens.

Breakfast was brought to her in bed, together with a carefully folded copy of *The Times*. Lady Denman apologised to her for the poverty of the arrangements, but she was 'short of staff'.

The first approach made to Vita to write the Handbook came on 20 May 1943, when a Miss Bower and a Miss Parry journeyed to Sissinghurst. They first tried to persuade her to travel all over Britain to gather the information on behalf of the Ministry of Agriculture, to which request they received a definite *no*. Though in carrying out her duties she was motivated by a blend of patriotism, and a deep love of the countryside, she was, nevertheless, a busy writer of articles and books, as well as a notable broadcaster. This, coupled with the running of Sissinghurst, (where she employed two WLA girls), and family commitments besides, already made considerable demands on her. However, by October, she had finally agreed to do the book, and began writing it in November 1943, but not, Nigel Nicolson records, 'with any great pleasure', since it was to be an official publication. Much of the book, *The Women's Land Army*, was based on Vita's own local experiences and knowledge of farming. She did, nevertheless, receive help from Headquarters, which sent not only official brochures but also copies of letters, and transcripts of broadcasts by Land Girls. As agreed, she did not have to travel the British Isles in search of copy, rather meeting those she needed to see in London: representatives of the Welsh WLA on 7 October 1943; Donald McCullough, at the Ministry of Agriculture, in November (to hear details of the 'Empire Discussion' and of the many other radio broadcasts with which Mr McCullough was involved); and lunch with Mrs Stevenson of the Women's Timber Corps the following January. As the Minister of Agriculture, Robert Hudson, was a personal friend, and her cousin, the Earl De La Warr, had been Parliamentary Secretary at the Ministry of Agriculture in 1935, it is likely that she would also have discussed the WLA with them. The finished draft was ready by the middle of March, when Lady Denman and Mrs Pyke lunched at Sissinghurst to discuss it with her. Finally, after revisions, the book was published on 25 September 1944. As she feared, it had turned into an uncertain combination of recruiting document, and historical record of WLA administration and membership. She had attempted to counteract this by including something of the uncomfortable side of Land Army life, making reference to the volunteer's 'damp boots, her reeking oil-skin, and the mud and numbing cold'; observing that:

> It would be absurd to pretend that everything in the Land Army had invariably been perfect, and that the conduct of every girl had been model, heroic, and in every way beyond reproach. Such a contention would carry no conviction and would tend only to diminish any further record of the very real merit of the majority.

Dry though the book may have appeared to her, it is certain that none of the other services is able to lay claim to such philosophy and writing excellence as that which appears in *The Women's Land Army*:

> Whenever one is dealing with human beings in the mass, some very odd and unforeseen factors emerge. They are most revealing, and demonstrate how much at fault one was in any preconceived estimate of how people are likely to react in given circumstances. Thus it was astonishing to find that one-third of the Land Army volunteers came from London or our large industrial cities; and astonishing to note the tragic disappointment shown by those who

Londoners signing on as members of the WLA at a makeshift recruiting office near a burnt-out building.

could not be accepted for country work because they were more urgently needed elsewhere. This surprising fact does suggest that there are many townspeople who feel they would prefer the country, in complete contradiction to the popular view that the youth of to-day is wedded to the cities.

It is claimed by admirers of Vita Sackville-West's writing that there was rather more of Lady Denman in the text than might be immediately obvious to the uninitiated. Indeed, the writer H. J. Massingham, who had initially, and somewhat critically,

87

reviewed the book at its face value, wrote to its author in December 1944, craving forgiveness, but adding:

> I can't help smiling at the unnerving way I picked out Lady Denman's contributions, being more right than I knew in saying - how could an artist like Miss Sackville-West descend to such jargon!?

Profits from the sale of the book were given to the WLA Benevolent Fund, and Robert Lusty, a director of Michael Joseph, the book's publishers, was able to write to Vita in August 1945, informing her that a sum of £1,039 3s. 4d. had been sent to the Fund, adding:

> I think The Women's Land Army should be well pleased with this result, and I hope they will realise how very much they owe to you for the enormous amount of tedious work you did for them.

It is worth noting that when Lady Denman wrote to thank her for her efforts with the Handbook, she addressed Vita as 'The Hon. Mrs Harold Nicolson', a form of address Vita was universally known to loathe, refusing to submerge her identity beneath her husband's name.

Vita Sackville-West's last connection with the WLA was in June 1945, a week after she had finished as District Representative, when she attended a rally at Canterbury, presided over by the Duchess of Kent. Despite her initial lack of enthusiasm for the project, *The Women's Land Army*, remains a unique account of what it meant to be a member of the WLA. Her final contribution on behalf of the Benevolent Fund was to write the Foreword to *Poems of the Land Army*, an anthology of members' poems.

The pages of *The Land Girl* served many purposes, and one was to record the success of fund-raising efforts for the Spitfire Funds. The Funds stemmed from a query in a Jamaican newspaper as to the cost of building a bomber for the RAF, the answer to which was £20,000. A week later the Ministry of Aircraft Production received an anonymous cheque for that amount. The idea caught the public imagination, and soon similar collections were started throughout Britain and the Empire. A less expensive aircraft, such as a Spitfire, had a price-tag of £5,000 and a city or group contributing this amount could 'buy' one. The suggestion that the WLA should have its own Fund came in September 1940, when, as the *The Land Girl* informed its readers, this 'excellent notion' was put forward by several members, among them Miss Elizabeth Cross of West Sussex:

> It would be exciting to think that one of the many fighters that roar about over our heads while we are at work might be our very own. After all, it's not much good us getting corns on our hands and aching backs growing food if a lot of Nazis turn up to eat it!

Rallies were one way to get Land Army members together.
Lady Denman *(third from left)* liked to attend as many as possible. She is seen here
accompanying Lady Spencer *(centre)*, Chairman of the Northamptonshire WLA,
at one such gathering in October 1940.

The Land Girl carried a progress report that November:

> The Spitfire Fund has now reached £361, a good beginning, but so far
> only a beginning ... we must work a little harder to make our own [Fund]
> a big success.

This may seem now to have been overly optimistic. The women received a small
wage, and there were numerous other demands on the few pounds they were able
to save; but this was wartime, and *The Land Girl* compiled a list of ingenious WLA
collecting methods:

> Hostel dances, losses at bridge and other games, sale of blackberries, hop-
> picking, and the exhibition of a frog at a halfpenny a view have been the
> means of raising funds, while several volunteers have sent a week's (one
> even a month's) rise money.

One issue of the *Kent News Sheet*, reported that a very successful dance at the

89

Canterbury Co-operative Hall, had raised £8 for the Spitfire Fund, and in addition, 'the whole proceeds of the ladies cloakroom' were also contributed to the Fund!

By the 8 August 1941 the Fund had reached its goal of £5,000. In celebration, a luncheon was organised in London at the Carlton Grill, in Pall Mall, although who paid for it remains a mystery - possibly it was Lady Denman, since she seemed to pay for just about everything else. As Huntingdonshire and Worcestershire had contributed most to the total, a representative from each of these counties was chosen to hand over the cheque. The WLA representative for Huntingdonshire remembers that it was a 'very posh do', and recorded details of the lunch in her diary:

> Smoked salmon, hors d'oevres, chicken, and macaroni cheese, raspberries and raspberry ice cream, and all washed down by beer. In view of the fact that we are completing the second full year of war, I feel we did well.

The Land Girl's editor, Margaret Pyke, continued to applaud members' efforts on behalf of the Fund, and to encourage greater efforts still. But, as Angus Calder records in his book *The People's War*:

> The Spitfire Funds . . . were a largely spontaneous outflow of public opinion, which Beaverbrook's propagandist flair turned to striking effect. The idea was that the people paid for their own Spitfires. In sober truth, money was now quite irrelevant to the production of fighters; but the pennies and pounds which were contributed had a useful anti-inflationary effect.

If *The Land Girl* served the essential function of creating a sense of identity and purpose for its members, the organisation both of County, and sometimes National, Rallies was effective and enjoyable. Saturday afternoons were a favourite time, and all registered WLA members in a given area were invited. One such Rally, in Cambridge, in April 1941, was attended by Mrs Joan Marshall, a WLA Volunteer:

> We assembled at Parker's Piece, about seventy in all. The band of the Home Guard joined us, looking very smart in khaki uniforms. We marched through Cambridge to 'Keep the Home Fires Burning' and other marching airs. The parade ended at the Guildhall where we were received by the Mayor. Lady Grey, Lady Denman, and two farmers addressed us, and Lady Denman gave us our badges. Compliments from the farmers were quoted. After the presentations we had a really lovely tea of dainty little sandwiches and fancy cakes, to which I did full justice!

Occasionally, if the County Chairman was so-minded, the girls would be invited for a summer party at her house, or the wife of a suitable owner be persuaded to

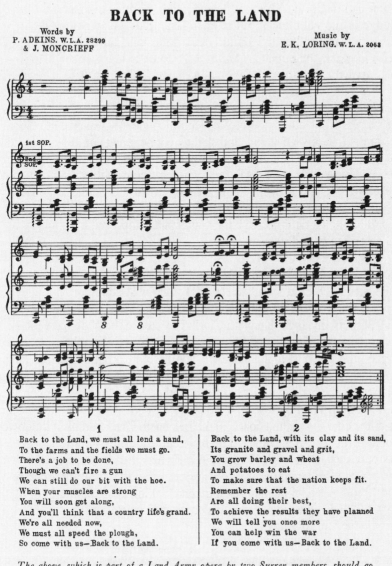

BACK TO THE LAND

Words by
P. ADKINS. W.L.A. 28299
& J. MONCRIEFF

Music by
E. K. LORING. W. L. A. 2053

1

Back to the Land, we must all lend a hand,
To the farms and the fields we must go.
There's a job to be done,
Though we can't fire a gun
We can still do our bit with the hoe.
When your muscles are strong
You will soon get along,
And you'll think that a country life's grand.
We're all needed now,
We must all speed the plough,
So come with us—Back to the Land.

2

Back to the Land, with its clay and its sand,
Its granite and gravel and grit,
You grow barley and wheat
And potatoes to eat
To make sure that the nation keeps fit.
Remember the rest
Are all doing their best,
To achieve the results they have planned
We will tell you once more
You can help win the war
If you come with us—Back to the Land.

*The above, which is part of a Land Army opera by two Surrey members, should go
with a swing at Land Army parties. Single Copies 1d. each, 2d. post free, or 12
for 1s., post free, can be obtained from the Editor.*

'Back to the Land'
The anthem of the Women's Land Army during the Second World War.

organise an estate tour, with afternoon tea as a bonus. Some enterprising County Chairmen arranged agricultural outings to Research Stations, Colleges, or Farm Institutes. This was designed not so much to extend the working knowledge of the volunteers, but to encourage that elusive *esprit de corps*.

'At parties and rallies the Land Army Song is usually sung' wrote W. E. Shewell-Cooper in the *Land Girl Manual*. 'It is easy to learn, cheerful to sing and helps to create the right spirit.' Sing-songs played, as they still do, a large part in any Women's Land Army gathering, and the creation of their 'very own' song was a matter of considerable pride to its members.

The success of the attempt to create a common identity was in part responsible for the carefree, happy-go-lucky, and slightly comic, image of the Land Girl that persists to the present day - an image, indeed, acknowledged by many members themselves. It was difficult, too, for those whose responsibility it was to record the images of war to perceive the work of women in the fields, or of domestic agricultural labour as such, as having the same visual force as war in the cities or on the battlefield. Agriculture, like the countryside, appeared to represent an unchanging continuity and stability.

The importance of a discernable visual image, both through newsreel and in art, had been recognised during the First World War, although artists like Randolph Schwabe, and Archibald Standish Hartrick, who wished to portray the woman landworker were scarce. By 1939 it might have been assumed that things were different, particularly as Sir Kenneth Clark, Director of the National Gallery, and Controller Home Publicity in the Ministry of Information, was able to persuade the Ministry to support the idea of a War Artists Advisory Committee, which included representatives of the Royal College of Art, and the Slade School of Fine Art, where Randolph Schwabe had been Professor of Painting. Some financial support for the project came from The Pilgrim Trust, which encouraged works of art and historical records of the countryside and coast. Had Sir Kenneth Clark had his way, however, it is probable that few paintings would have been commissioned showing landworkers, or female landworkers in particular. He had already expressed the opinion that 'the trouble about war paintings of agriculture is that they are rather hard to distinguish from peace-time pictures.' Anyone looking at the paintings of agriculture, however, and at the women workers portrayed in them, can only wonder at the short-sightedness of this view.

For the many sympathetic paintings of women land workers, and the Women's Land Army, by Evelyn Dunbar, we are, according to art historian, Demelza Spargo, in the debt of Lady Norman, a Trustee of the Imperial War Museum.

Early in December 1939, Lady Norman made a firm request for the inclusion of this category of work in subjects to be covered by the project. She believed that such paintings could provide an important comparison with the works produced during the Great War.

In March, 1940, the Ministry of Information published a list of the artists they had commissioned, including those who were to depict the civilian effort on the land. Among these were Mona Moore, Archibald Hartrick, Nora Lavrin, James Bateman, Evelyn Dunbar and Thomas Hennell, all of whom, as Demelza Spargo writes:

> Covered a wide range of agricultural subjects in works which demonstrated clear stylistic differences from those works produced during World War 1. On the strength of such results the Ministry of Agriculture urged the War Artists Committee to authorise greater coverage of agricultural topics, but the response, sadly, was that of Sir Kenneth Clark . . . [this] would suggest that from time immemorial, and stretching infinitely into the future, paintings of work on the land would consist of a similar approach to the subject, any variation being related purely to individual artistic style or to period or national style. Such an interpretation is restrictively narrow and severs all connections between the painting and the time in which it was made.

For the Land Girls, in spite of the war artists, their lasting image was not to be that of dignified labour in the fields, nor of women going about their business in serious enjoyment, but rather a glamorised, or a comic cartoon version. Perhaps, though, this is more representative of the way in which many volunteers saw themselves.

'Girl Milking', by Evelyn Dunbar (1906-60).
In 1939 Evelyn Dunbar was sent to Sparsholt Agricultural College in Hampshire to produce paintings for the WAAC where she painted several works on dairy practice.

7
Each To Their Own
Recollections of the Second Women's Land Army

It was astonishing to find that one-third of the Land Army volunteers came from London or our large industrial cities; and astonishing to note the tragic disappointment shown by those who could not be accepted for country work because they were more urgently needed elsewhere. This surprising fact does suggest that there are many townspeople who feel they would prefer the country, in complete contradiction to the popular view that the youth of today is wedded to the cities
Introduction to The Women's Land Army, *1944.*

From an early age, I had loved anything to do with farming, especially the animal side of it - pigs, cows, and chickens, and of course the horses. On leaving school in 1929 I went to Studley College, in Warwickshire, which catered for 'Women Only' in those days. I took the general two-year course which consisted of dairying: including butter and cheese-making; and stock management: including poultry, pigs and sheep. In those days not much modern machinery was available. In fact the milking machine was only installed during my last term, in 1931. Neither were there any drinking troughs for the cows. They were put in a few years later. We had, in all, about forty milking cows and six of us - plus the cowman - all started milking the hard way by 6 a.m. on the dot. In the winter when the cows were in at night four of us were on evening shift to give the cows a late-night drink of water, and so keep up milk production. We were told they drank at least two gallons of water to each gallon of milk, or thereabouts. It was illegal to water the milk, so we had to water the cows instead! As the 'shippens' were anything but modern we had to make sure the cows were all lying on clean, dry, straw before leaving.

After leaving Studley, where we even ploughed with horses, [I was] still living at Burley, in the New Forest, when I got a job. It was on a big poultry farm: over 5,000 birds from day olds to two years old; we also bought in turkeys for Christmas.

Two days a week we delivered eggs to various hotels and private houses in Southampton. Also table birds. We started delivery about 8.30 a.m. and went on solidly until 3 p.m., getting back to the farm near Ringwood about 4 p.m. Then all the paraffin lamps in the broiler houses had to be seen to, and water, mash, and corn distributed. Then I had to cycle back to Burley - about four miles up and down hill.

I had all my meals at the farm, including breakfast, and was paid 30s. a week. I thought I was well done by! After a few years on the same farm, I decided to move on, and sold a pearl necklace to buy my first Jersey cow, and a breeding sow. I also had a New Forest Pony which I broke in, and showed in 1938 as a four year old.

Then, in 1939, I was called up as a VAD. So I sold the cow and pigs, and off I went to the RVH at Netley. After over a year there the urge to get back to the land came over me again, and, as my mother and sister had by then gone to Cornwall, I was allowed to join the Land Army. My first job was on a general farm, mostly dairying, plus acres of potatoes, and good old Cornish broccoli. Then I met someone whose farm had been taken over as a training centre for the Land Army. When he heard I had been to Studley . . . he recommended me as an Assistant County Dairy instructress. This I did for three years, which was just when they wanted the Cornish farmers to stop making cream, as the need for liquid milk was more urgent. This was none too easy as most of the farms were occupied by tenants, and with hardly any water laid on. The standard of cleanliness left much to be desired. However, I found that with this job it was ninety-eight per cent tact and two per cent knowledge which was needed, and I visited about forty or fifty farms all-told, and eventually got most of them up to standard. In fact my worst farm became a really first-class clean milk producer, with automatic recorders. I enjoyed that job, and felt I had achieved something.

By that time, with the Second Front looming, I was duly sent back to Netley, and eventually to Italy. After the war was over I married. My husband and I had a smallholding right in the middle of Bodmin Moor, below Jamaica Inn. We kept a few cows and pigs, and finally returned to the New Forest with three children, and another pony which I drove for many years.

I. Passy, Brockenhurst, Hampshire.

At the beginning of 1940 I went to London, and enrolled with the Women's Land Army. The lady there asked me if I was afraid of cows, and, as I was full of patriotic fervour at the time, I lied, and said no!

Shortly after that, rigged out in corduroy breeches, green pullover, felt hat, heavy shoes, and long woollen socks, I was on a train bound for Peterborough to be met by the farmer who was to employ me. I only stayed with him a few weeks, as it became obvious that he only wanted Land Army girls for cheap labour, coupled with very long working hours. He also had six obnoxious children!

So I moved on further, into the flat, seemingly endless landscape of the Fens. My next employer was a kind, pink-faced man named Charlie, who was married to an inefficient ex-housemaid, years older than himself. Both he and his wife were completely dominated by his fearsome old mother. My job was to help with the milking of forty cows, morning and afternoon. After breakfast I drove the little Ford van around the nearby small town selling the milk. The customers were often quite offended when I insisted they paid for their supply of milk. It seemed one didn't pay Charlie - they had been at school with him! During the time I worked there I must have collected several hundreds of pounds which were owing him.

I loved the cows, after I had conquered my initial nervousness. I loved their dignified walk, their gentle eyes, and lovely long eyelashes. They always knew which stall to walk into after being out on the Wash pastures; they knew which of their sisters they stood next to, and immediately backed out if they found they had gone wrong. They all had a friend to be with when grazing in the fields. 'White Socks' could always be found near 'Betty', and so on. They were a mongrel herd, so we had no 'high falutin' names, but most of them knew the names Charlie had given them, and came when called. 'Connie' was the most maternal. She had had thirteen calves, and loved them all. She once struggled across a dyke to a calf not her own which had become separated from its mother. There were horses on the farm, but I had little to do with them. We had at least three very hard winters during the War, and standing around 'topping' mangolds, and cleaning the mud off them on a frosty afternoon was not much fun, and yet, curiously, it was during those years that I stopped having chilblains. Life had its lighter moments. Another Land Girl working nearby had been a beauty specialist, employed in Bond Street, before the War. On meeting her, one diabolically cold morning when it was sleeting freezing rain, she greeted me with the words: 'Oh, deah - my face is in *ribbons*!!'

If one was not too tired in the evenings there were Farmers Union dances or the local cinema. My landlady was a buxom, jolly country woman with a robust and earthy sense of humour. She was a great joy to me, and I laughed more in her company than ever before or since.

After three years of dairy farming I had to have a rest, because, as Sam the cowman said, 'Every day comes reg'lar, Missis.' I was then seconded to the Milk Marketing Board as a Milk Recorder, the job I did until the end of the War. One hair-raising day, I was very nearly machine-gunned by one of our own pilots who was chasing an enemy bomber. The German was trying, in broad daylight, to locate the place where ammunition was hidden and stored, and our man was heading him off. Down below, I was innocently delivering the milk. I scuttled into a nearby doorway as a series of bullets scuttered along the garden path I had so recently walked up. We were not issued with tin hats in the Isle of Ely, as were the Kentish Land Girls. No doubt their need was greater than ours!

Phyllis Cunningham, Darsham, Suffolk.

I was in the WLA from 1940-4, and joined because I wanted 'to do my bit' but didn't want the strictness of the services. I had always had a love of the country. I was first sent to a Horticultural College for one month, where we had many different jobs to do for one week at a time. I well remember after the first week when we started milking we could hardly hold knives and forks. The next week it was pigs, and we had a rather fierce boar. One of us used to dangle some pig swill in a bucket on the end of a belt while [Peggy] climbed over the fence to tip the other bucketful into the trough. Unfortunately, she often didn't make it back and the boar bit her bottom! As well, at the College, I remember our indignation at having to disbud chrysanthemums in the rain. We didn't see that was helping the war effort.

I was then sent to a lonely farm with a very elderly owner of eighty-six, and her companion (fifty-six), plus one farm worker. We had kippers and porridge every morning for breakfast. We had forty cows which had to be taken over two miles every day down to the marshes where they got into other peoples fields, and all went the wrong way. During the first week I was cleaning out the pigsty and let the pigs out. They ran all round the village. I wasn't very popular after that, and was sent to a big market-garden farm. I liked this very much. We used to work with horses, and there were also fifteen to twenty Land Girls from all walks of life. We used to start work at 6.30 a.m., which was very hard if you had been up all night with air raids, and stopped work at 8.30 a.m. for breakfast. As soon as we sat down in the fields so the air raid warnings would go, and we used to see the Spitfires and Hurricanes take off. We were near Gravesend Airport, right where the Battle of Britain took place, and we watched dog fights in the air. If we went into town in the evening the last bus used to leave at 8 p.m., so we had to catch a bus to the edge of town and walk the rest of the way - three or four miles: no joke, with bombs and shrapnel falling around you! I met my future husband on this farm, as he was on a searchlight camp. But he was moved around, and so was I. I worked on numerous farms, and learned to drive a tractor, and later a car, so that I went on a milk round. We often got forced into a ditch by heavy army lorries.

We were sent hop-picking, which was great fun, as the Londoners were camping in hop huts and had camp fires. We had to have a sub of our wages to pay our landladies, as hop-pickers only got paid at the end of the season. On another farm we were opening a field of corn with hand scythes, and had left our satchels with food and flasks at the side. Some pigs got to them, and ate all our lovely home-made meat pies! Our landlady was a marvellous cook.

I helped with the sheep on another farm: docking lambs' tails, and castrating them, then going round to see if they were all right; [as well as] sheep dipping, and shearing; helping to get the corn in, and building the stacks. Very frightening, when you are in a little hole and they are building the roof, but I wouldn't have changed it for anything. Both my husband and I have very fond memories of the war.

Barbara White, Swanscombe, Kent.

I was the eldest of three girls, and at twenty, all women were expected to do some useful work for the war effort. As I was a shop assistant this was not considered to be important. The WRNS was full, and also the WRAF, and I didn't like the idea of factory work in an enclosed space, so I decided to join the WLA, and I have never regretted it.

My friend and I were offered a job in Dorset doing field work. We were to join twenty more girls at Leeds station, and all travel down to Manston Hostel near Sturminster Newton on the 2 March, 1942. We were met at Sturminster Newton station, and taken to the Hostel, which was about a mile away.

The Hostel was quite unlike home life we had been used to, with about thirty girls in the dormitory, and double wooden bunks to sleep on, and a wardrobe and locker for our clothes. We shared a dining/sitting room, a wash room with showers, wash basins, and a couple of baths and toilets. We were all given a bicycle, which we found quite difficult to handle as they were heavy. Our first job was cutting back hedges, and cleaning out ditches. We didn't have any accidents apart from getting our boots stuck in the mud, trying to release them - losing our balance and sitting down - or just leaving them behind. On one of our cycle rides to work we went over the bridge, at Sturminster Newton, where we turned right. One girl didn't quite make it, and went straight into someone's front door. The door flew open but Winnie dragged the bicycle back, shut the door, and we continued on our way!

Haymaking and hoeing proved very tiring. On returning to the Hostel in the evening we felt too tired even to eat. The local people were suspicious when we first arrived, and of course some of the girls had no intention of working. About three months after we arrived our twenty-first birthdays came, so we managed to have a few parties, as we had parcels of food, and presents from home. Whilst we were at the Hostel one of the girls was injured when the bicycle she was riding was in collision with a wall, after her brakes failed. She died later in hospital.

Volunteers were asked for driving tractors, rat catching, and making thatch with a machine. I was told that I was too small to drive a tractor, so my friend and I went to Sixpenny Handley to make thatch. I did later drive a tractor; it was a Fordson Standard, which I enjoyed driving. I also travelled to Corfe Castle, Dorchester, and Rampisham. At a farm, just outside Toller Porcorum, we did some threshing. The elevator had a cracked casting, and the foreman asked the men to hold it together so that the elevator could be wound down. They refused, so we girls were told to do it; unfortunately it came down rather more quickly than we anticipated, and my head was jammed between two lengths of wood. I saw a doctor after being released, but he seemed to think I was all right! Another accident happened when a trailer overturned. It was being pulled by a tractor towing two trailers, and resulted in a fatal injury for another girl. One day we were travelling back from threshing at Beaminster when the lorry in which we were riding left the road, and finished up in a ditch, but, apart from a few bruises, this time we were all unhurt. I left the Land Army to get married in 1945.

Mary Coombes, Dorchester, Dorset.

My father thought that only girls of dubious morals joined the ATS and WAAFS. The WRNS offered me a job in the cookhouse, which infuriated me, so I joined the Land Army as the only thing left. I was informed that I was considered suitable for a place at a College of Horticulture in Cheshire, and would be notified. I was thrilled.

Alas, time went on, so I wrote and suggested that I was found a job whilst I waited. Immediately I was told to report to a private house in Lydney, Gloucestershire. Not knowing, in my innocence, that I was now in the 'servant class', I knocked on the imposing front door. I was told to go round to the tradesmen's entrance, and was then taken to meet the gardener. He scowled, thrust a hoe into my hand, waved vaguely at a plot of land, and said "Oe it awff.' I hacked at everything in sight; it was autumn, so everything looked dead to me. I don't know how much damage I did, but the local pub heard all about it that night! I lodged with a kind family in the village, and they were angry about this. It was their support which kept me going in the next miserable weeks.

The late autumn of 1941 was a cold, frosty one. Just the time to dig up the tennis court! I arrived home exhausted and blistered. My landlady ran me a bath immediately, and, with some home-made bread and jam inside me, packed me off to bed. That was the daily routine, as I worked side by side with that man until it was done. I would do it if it killed me! I only saw my employer on a Friday. The small sum was written on a cheque, and then placed with a packet of cigarettes by his hand so that I had to come within reaching distance. How I dreaded that weekly humiliation.

Living in a tiny terrace cottage, my bedroom spartan and unheated, I had to be with my hosts a great deal. The nights were dark. I knew no one, as the other few land girls were dotted about the Forest, and we only met together occasionally at our supervisor's home. I couldn't stay in every evening. I felt that these kind people needed a little time together when their two small boys were put to bed. Apart from the cinema there was a canteen run by some women at the Church Hall - tea and buns, table tennis and Ludo! The boys came down from their lonely anti-aircraft sites, and, as there were no servicewomen in the area, found me! Little did I know that my somewhat boring evening, and the short walk home up the main street with a chivalrous escort, was giving me a *reputation*. When the Vicar's wife called on my landlady one afternoon, and poured out her disgust, she was furious. It really did seem to be time for a change.

I had a meeting with Lady Bathurst, who was in charge of the whole area, and asked if I could be put somewhere large enough to get lost in. I had paid a visit to Cheltenham on a day off, and found it charming. So when she offered me a place there, I accepted. She said that they had had a succession of girls who had been put in very inferior accommodation, but had been warned that this would be the last girl. So it turned out, as I stayed there until the end of the war, before going to College. I worked in the grounds of a private hotel, and had a room in the hotel and excellent food. Again, I was put with the servants - and treated as such by the residents. I was always amused by their offended looks when I refused a tip for rendering some small service. I wasn't behaving correctly in their scheme of things!

The gardener and a boy looked after the fruit and vegetables. My job was to look after an assortment of fowls, rabbits, and usually one cow in calf. When the feeding, cleaning, and milking had been done, I helped wherever I was needed. In the late summer and autumn I took the surplus fruit and tomatoes to market. This meant pushing a handcart about two miles down a busy main road, and through the town. When the hotel was taken over by the Americans, for senior officers, my social life improved, too!

When I look back, I do feel that we were treated badly. After paying for my digs, I had so little left. I had to save for weeks to buy a book. I remember going into the YMCA for a meal. I thought I could afford beans on toast until I realised that I had to pay a shilling for a knife and fork! The YMCA in Salisbury turned me away as I was not 'in the Services'. When my boots were beyond repair the Army sent me some second-hand ones - I wasn't due for new ones. My goodness they hurt! When I walked down the aisle of the village church and was 'shushed', as my horseshoe heels rang on the gratings, I felt hurt and angry. Looking after animals, I worked long hours. On summer evenings I always had to come back before dusk to look at the fowls. That was for six and a half days a week. But in those days we complained little, and never thought about 'rights'. One thing I did realise: work like this was useful, but not for me. I was now twenty-one, and needed something to act as a spur. The opportunity to go to a College of Education came at the right moment, and I wallowed in being able to use my brain after using my hands. Oh, and I did get tossed by a cow!

Dorothy Pilson, Cheltenham, Gloucestershire.

I was in the WLA from 1940-6, so I felt I did my stint! Firstly, my reasons for joining were that I had just left school, and was about to start at a PT College (now called P. E. - Physical Education). I was aged seventeen years when I heard the Princess Royal appeal on the radio for girls to join the Land Army and so release the men to join up. Without more ado I rushed to the Labour Exchange, said I was eighteen (the minimum age for the WLA), and signed up. Three months later - I thought I would have gone the next week! - I was sent to Sparsholt Agricultural Institute, near Winchester, for one month's training, specialising (if you can call it that) in tractor driving. I enjoyed that month, and meeting other girls. Having been away at boarding school it didn't worry me to leave home, but quite a few of the girls were homesick. I often wonder how many of that intake lasted the war.

It was August 1940, and the time of 'dog fights' in the air during the Battle of Britain, a great many of which we saw. After our training, jobs were difficult to find as farmers were reluctant to employ a girl in place of a man. But, after a month at home - when I felt I should have joined the WRNS, and been appreciated - I was sent to a job in Somerset. I only stayed one month as my job there was to groom the horses, comb the English sheepdogs, and do the housework. We also had to stand up every Sunday evening while the National Anthems of all the Allies were played on the radio, and each Sunday the list got longer!

I felt this was not war-work, and not the job I joined up to do. I then had five months in the Forestry Corps in Wareham, Dorset, billeted with the YWCA. My eyes were certainly opened there: what a tough bunch! But I met some very nice

101

girls, one of whom left with me in 1941 to work on a nearby farm, and we stayed together until we were demobbed in 1946. In 1940, at Wareham, I also met a young army officer - the week of my eighteenth (supposedly nineteenth!) birthday, and we were eventually married five years later, in October 1945. After our honeymoon, I returned to the Land Army job, which by this time was contract tractor-driving in West Dorset, and my husband joined his army unit in Germany.

We really were a forgotten army. I feel that we *were* neglected. No one seemed to take any notice of us; never visited us. We had no privileges. There was bad pay, no free travel, no use of canteens, and no gratuity. I still have the letter I sent to the WLA, with a drawing of Mr Chad saying, 'Wot, no gratuity?' It came back with, 'but 45 coupons', written on it.

Despite all, we survived, and no doubt were appreciated by the farmers, once they saw the work we could do - even cranking a tractor after it had been standing in a field all night in winter. We had our fun as well. At one place we used to go to army dances. Our bicycles were a *must*, even though we wore long skirts and had to tie them up with string so they wouldn't catch in the chain. One farmer allowed the three of us to organise dances in the Granary, and, as we had an Ack-Ack site on the farm, we had an army band and plenty of support. I also organised a mixed hockey match against the ATS and Gunners, playing in one of the farm fields. What with avoiding cowpats, and army sergeants, it was quite hilarious. A Land Girl I met during that last job is now Godmother to one of my daughters, and I still keep in contact with the couple I was billeted with in Netherbury, Dorset, and with many others. I was amused a short while ago to visit a small farm museum and to see there many of the tools we used in World War Two - antiques!

Barbara Ellis, Totnes, South Devon.

During the Second World War, I was a Land Army girl for almost four years, living in three different Hostels. During that time I made some wonderful friends. We lived together, and helped each other - had to. Of course, there were some bitchy girls. I remember my first night as a 'rookie'. In the lounge was an old wind-up gramophone, and one of the girls put on 'Home, Sweet Home'. I was feeling homesick anyway, and that did it. She was an 'old sweat', you see, with about a month behind her! I rushed to my bedroom, and wept. I was pleased I didn't have to share a room with that girl.

There were four girls to each bedroom, in a lovely old rectory. I made friends quickly and soon settled in. It was a hard life, thinking back . . . frozen hands in the winter when cutting beet; dusty and filthy from the threshing machine in summer - travelling from one farm to another with the machine, until each farmer had his corn threshed, cycling back to the Hostel each night, tired out; then having to share a bath with one of your mates because of the shortage of water, and trying desperately to get a gleam back into our hair - no conditioners in those days! But it was a good life. The Hostel ruling was to leave the sink and bath as you would wish to find it: clean! And, yes, you always filled up the big black kettle for the next girl, after you had used it. Most of us thought of each other, especially on those dreaded 'days of the month' - out in the cold fields, longing for a hot drink to ease the pains.

Of course, we couldn't please all the farmers all of the time but we did work hard, and couldn't wait for the harvest teas to arrive, always being ravenously hungry. Some of those farmers were good, and grateful for the work we did. We *were* needed, but didn't get the privileges the other services did. I do remember we were often referred to as 'bundles of wheat': not looking so chic as the Khaki and Blue jobs; and very rarely offered a seat on a packed train, [even though] we had paid for our train tickets - no passes for us! We received 28s. a week in wages, with 21s. stopped for board and keep. So we had 7s. left to buy underwear (with coupons, of course), and everything we needed - toileteries, travel, medicines, etc.

Sometimes we tried to save some money by hitching a lift home in all kinds of lorries, including sand lorries. I hate to think of how we did travel. Before we reached the main road we had to cycle about three miles, so we left our cycles at the pub on the main road for 6d., from Saturday afternoon until Sunday evening - hoping to hitch back to collect our cycles. The other route was to cycle to the station, about eight miles, downhill all the way; another 6d. to leave the cycle, and not so good a return journey on Sunday evening - uphill all the way, and thinking of home, and Mum's cooking. Soon it was Monday again, and off to another farm; hoping, as we went out to the cycle shed, that we didn't have a puncture - calamity!

Frances Draper, Market Harborough, Leicestershire.

I joined the Land Army at the beginning of 1941. I was very green, as I was a London girl, and had been working in Bourne & Hollingsworth in Oxford Street. I signed on for three years to go harvesting with a threshing gang, which I must admit I knew nothing about at all.

I will never forget my first day's work. I arrived home very tired and quite exhausted. I went straight upstairs to my room, where I had lodgings. The next thing I knew it was early morning. I was still dirty, dusty, and covered with pieces of straw. My landlady had just left me there!

Another time, we were sent to thresh some barley. Not a good job anyway, but we were informed that we had to kill all the rats we came across. Most of us being town girls it was really quite frightening. Still, kill the rats we did. We ended up the day with a huge pile of dead rats. Feeling very pleased with myself, I strolled over to the farmer and proudly told him 'There are your rats', expecting a pat on the back, and a big thank you. But to my amazement I was told: 'Yer not finished yet, me gal. Yer must cut off all their tails!'

'What on earth for?' I asked.

'Because I get 1d. per tail.' was his reply!

I had the devil's own job trying to persuade the other three girls to help me. But cut off their tails we did, and we counted them: over 200 rats! I still can't believe we killed all that number...

On another farm, I was asked by the farmer if I could build a rick. Not to be beaten, I said I would have a go. And, considering I was still 'one of them Londoners', they thought I was stupid. Anyway, I built my rick, and it seemed a pretty good one. All concerned agreed, so home I went, a very proud Land Girl. But, when I arrived back in the morning, there they all were . . . and no rick. It had decided to collapse in the night. Was my face red! But the farmer told me it was a jolly good effort. After all, I was only one of those 'Townie Gals'.

I married a farmer's son, and became a farmer's wife, with three sons and a daughter. Two of my sons work for us on our farm. I have been a farmer's wife for over 35 years now, and admit that I'm more used to all the goings-on on the farm. But in those early days it really was quite something. But I enjoyed every moment of my five years as a Land Girl.

Mrs Vera Bailey, Chichester, Sussex.

I lived in Horwich, Bolton in Lancashire. I left school at fourteen years of age, and had been a towel weaver in the local mill. I joined the Land Army in July 1941. I was sent to work for the Cambridge War Agricultural Committee. There were sixty girls from the industrial areas of Manchester and Liverpool. We were in a Hostel, in Swaffham Prior, near Burwell; a very great variety of girls. We worked around Cambridgeshire on the harvest, stooking corn, and picking peas and beans for cattle fodder. We worked on potato riddlers on Burwell Fens. We cut reeds, and helped reclaim some of the Fen land - digging out bog oaks. In June 1942, six of us transferred to the Timber Corps. This we enjoyed, going to Yorkshire, and Lincolnshire, where I met my husband. I remained in the Forestry until we were discharged in June 1946. I married in December 1946, having really enjoyed those years.

Phyllis Basham, Brandon, Suffolk.

It was towards the end of 1941 that I decided I ought to do something to aid the war effort. I was almost nineteen, and in a comfortable office job, living a cushioned life with my parents in a modern house on the outskirts of Nottingham . . . and I must confess that in the end it was the breeches, jumper, and jaunty hat of the girl in the poster advertising the WLA that won me over!

My papers arrived in February 1942, and I was to report to a farm in Lincolnshire, where I would receive a month's training in milking. I began to have a few niggling doubts. So far I had had only visions of myself tossing hay on to a wagon. When the family jokingly asked if I knew the difference between a cow and a bull, I replied that I didn't . . . such things were certainly not discussed by young girls in the early 1940s!

Arriving at my destination, I met my fellow Land Army recruit. I felt that she was at an advantage from the start, having lived in a Lincolnshire village all her life. We were billeted with one of the farm workers, and his wife. The first shock came on my first visit to the toilet. I thought every house in Great Britain had a flush toilet. Of course, I didn't expect it to be tiled from ceiling to floor, but to me that chain was an essential part of life! The bucket toilet was a loathsome thing to me - the two 'holes' seemed far worse than just one! That first evening a terrible feeling of homesickness came over me. What had I done? I listened expectantly to the Nine o'clock news on the wireless, hoping that in the period between boarding the train at Nottingham, and the news, an armistice would have been declared and I could scurry back to the comfortable home and flush toilet I had left!

The farm was a large one, with two dairy herds. Apparently two girls were trained each month, one at hand milking, and the other at machine milking, and we were left to decide which of us should do what. Christine, my fellow recruit, decided swiftly: she preferred the machines. Our days started at 6.30 a.m., and I shall never forget the misery of that first month. Up to that time, the nearest I had ever been to cows was viewing them from a railway carriage window *en route* to our annual two-week holiday by the sea, or occasionally in a distant field on a rare visit to the local countryside. At the end of the month, my cow ... was still not producing enough milk to colour the tea at an afternoon tea party! In truth, I was terrified of the animal, and couldn't seem to master the art of squeezing and pulling at the same time ... I was also extremely dispirited, and thoroughly fed up, being constantly told that the previous trainee was milking six cows morning and evening by the end of the months training. I was glad when I boarded the train which was to take me to my new posting at North Somercotes, on the Lincolnshire coast, ten miles from Louth. I was met at Louth station by the lady farmer's married son, who ran a haulage business. I eventually kept my cycle there, and thought nothing of cycling the ten miles to Louth to the pictures and back.

I was to live on the farm with the widowed lady farmer and assist with the general farm work. Over a cup of tea she gave me a run-down of the farm, and my duties. There were eight cows in milk, and they (the farm worker and herself) had not attempted to use the new milking machines installed just two weeks before. They had thought it advisable to await my arrival seeing that I had been instructed for the past month in the art of machine milking, and would, therefore, have expert knowledge, and be able to teach them all they needed to know! It was when she began enquiring as to what make of machine I had used that I had to break the news to her. I had never handled a machine. But, I hastened to add, I was willing to learn - anything, rather than hand milk. I subsequently learned from Christine that the WLA had mixed the two of us up. *She* was having to learn hand milking! It was when I visited the toilet that I decided that I must at all costs master the art of machine milking. This was where I belonged: the toilet had a chain! I felt quite light-headed with relief, and happier than I had done since leaving home.

Between the three of us we mastered the milking machines, and I was duly left in charge. My courage and expertise grew, and a quiet understanding developed between me and the cows. I looked forward to milking time, and even managed to do some hand milking. The art of mastering, and understanding, the Lincolnshire dialect came about as slowly as hand milking. I seemed to say nothing but

'Pardon?', knowing full-well that, when the phrase was repeated, I should be none the wiser. But gradually everything fell into place. I too referred to a field as a 'close', and a cart as a 'rully'. I learned how to 'drove' cattle; no more harrowing mistakes, like the time I was sent to fetch a cow who had escaped from the others and was contentedly eating at a haystack. The stack was fenced on three sides with barbed wire, so I ushered it on, confident it would see the opening and walk through it. I wasn't unduly bothered when she failed to notice the opening, and loped straight past. I walked behind her at a quicker pace, and the same thing happened again. I was beginning to feel annoyed. Never mind, round again. Third time lucky. Each time our pace quickened until, finally, no one could have told whether it was me chasing the cow, or the cow chasing me!

My lady farmer was very economy minded - weren't we all during the war years! We never had toilet paper; but I was surprised to find one day - after she had replenished the toilet paper box - a copy of the Methodist Hymn Book! Being a Methodist myself I was quite sorry when we reached the Index at the back of the book. I had thoroughly enjoyed the odd verse of 'Through the Night of Doubt and Sorrow', or 'He Who Would Valiant Be'!

I spent three and a half years in the WLA, tackling all types of farm work. My love of the countryside increased, and I never returned to town life. I look upon those years as some of the happiest of my life. I married a Lincolnshire lad, and we have raised a country-loving Lincolnshire family.

Mary Smith, South Elkington, Lincolnshire.

I was a member of the Surrey Land Club which functioned during World War Two. The members mostly worked in offices or banks during the week, but at weekends went to Surrey farms and market gardens to do unskilled work. We did anything, from weeding minute onions, to pulling up and heaping mangol wurzels, or grovelling in mud for potatoes. It was all very back-breaking - hoeing most of all - but also fun. For this, we earned 6d. per hour, increasing to 9d., and I believe, eventually to one shilling. But all the money went to the Red Cross. We were, however, given a few clothing coupons, and got suitable clothes and gum boots. We took picnic lunches, and mostly arrived on bicycles, but sometimes we were collected at a railway station by lorry. Some farmers watched to see that we were giving them their money's worth, but many made us copious pots of tea and were most grateful for our hard labour.

Barbara Blake, Bridport, Dorset

I was in the Land Army from 1941-4. I was discharged because I lost my right leg in a threshing machine.

N. Archer, West Wickham, Kent.

8
Timber!

Many people would not believe that women could, or would, take the place of men.
Experience during the past three years has triumphantly proved how wrong they
were. All honour to the girls who, as volunteers, faced exile from home, the cold and
mud of winter, long hours and heavy work, to do a job of first importance for their
country.
Director of the Home Timber Production Department, Ministry of Supply, 1945.

The idea of the Women's Timber Corps was born in April 1942. The country's
woodlands had been severely and indiscriminately plundered during the First
World War, and although, by 1939, 600,000 acres of new woodland had been
planted these were far from mature. Timber is a vital munition in war. Between 1916
and 1917 there had been a deliberate German submarine campaign aimed at timber
imports, to prevent pit props in particular arriving at coal mines. Pits required an
almost inexhaustible supply of timber, and, with mining temporarily boosted in the
national need, it was to home production that the Ministry of Supply turned.
Needless to say, the available supply of manpower was insufficient for the
minimum requirements of the Forestry Commission, whose job it would be to fell
and transport the timber. Most worrying of all, how could the nursery work needed
to rear and plant new trees keep pace with the drain of the Commission's men, who
were being drafted from civilian duties to the military? Census work was also
needed in order to assess the standing woodlands of England and Wales, and to
continue the 'flying census' that had been conducted in Scotland in 1941. Endless
measuring and stocktaking were necessary, and ultimately, felling, haulage, and
sawmill operations. So the familiar appeal went out to women. They were needed
not just on the farms, but also in the sawmills, forests, and the woodland nurseries.

The Forestry Commission had been established in 1919, in order to relieve the
newly-created Ministry of Agriculture of its responsibilities for timber. In 1917, the
Government had apppointed a Forestry Sub-Committee, under the Chairmanship
of Sir Francis Acland, and out of this came the Forestry Act, 1919, which established

a Commission with powers and aims, but without a single tree or an acre of land to its name.

Remarkably, the Forestry Commission had succeeded, between the wars, in planting an average of some 30,000 acres a year, but by the start of the Second World War much of the wood for pit props, telegraph poles, and the like, was still imported. Now home-produced timber became an immediate necessity. Forestry's proximity to agriculture denied it any of the wartime advantages or privileges accruing to manufacturing, and instead output was dependent upon whatever inexperienced hand accepted the quite exceptional demands of the business.

Though, nominally, the Women's Timber Corps was a single organisation, in practice there were two: one for Scotland, and one for England and Wales. In Scotland, where the Land Army was controlled not from Balcombe but by the Department of Agriculture for Scotland, women had already been working as measurers since the outbreak of the war. Here, a Women's Forestry Service (WFS) had been formed at the beginning of 1941, and many of the WFS members had taken part in the 1941 'flying census' - a government attempt to establish the extent of the timber resource by cataloguing stands of timber above five acres. In practice, it proved impossible to measure every stand. In his evocative, unpublished book, 'Beating about the Bush', George Ryle observed:

> As foresters we were all rather ashamed of ourselves for the very crudeness of this flying survey, but it would be better to have a rough and ready schedule of our overall resources than precise data as to a small fraction of them and nothing about the remainder.

The enthusiastic Mr Ryle, as famous for his indiscretion as for his energy, was with the Commission from 1924 to 1977, and in daily contact with hundreds of WTC members during the war years. He always extended to them the highest praise:

> There was the lady bank cashier from Kent, quiet, reserved, a calm disciplinarian, whose standard of work, stock returns and despatches had to be 100% accurate. There was the lady from the West End beauty parlour who had had tragedy in her life but whose sole objective was to maintain productivity in her mill just a little bit higher than anyone else's.

To extend the census nearly one thousand new members were recruited from the Land Army of England and Wales, and they formed the second half of the new Corps which was seconded to the Home Timber Production Department of the Ministry of Supply. It had proved impossible to measure every stand of timber in Scotland, and, as the woodlands of England and Wales were even less uniform and, on average, considerably smaller, women were not simply 'wanted' they were *indispensible*. The extension of the Scottish survey, using the sampling method, would have been impossible had the Commission had to rely on its existing workforce.

Members of the new national Corps were recruited mainly from the towns, and then transferred to camps near the woods, where they received a modest issue of working kit. In Scotland, where the main demand for workers lay in felling, and preparing pitwood, training was concentrated on general forest work. At the training camps all volunteers would have the opportunity to learn sawmill work, and haulage, using both horses and tractors. In England and Wales, where the demand was more varied, specialised training was provided. For the first week of any training course recruits were introduced to the four main sections of the work: felling, cross-cutting, clearing in the woods (which involved sawing and measuring), tractor driving and haulage. For the remainder of the course each woman could specialise. Only two hundred of the nucleus of one thousand founding members of the Women's Timber Corps for England and Wales had any previous experience of measuring. 'Girls could not be expected to learn all the tricks of the trade in a month', ran the Introduction to *Meet the Members* (an official tribute to the WTC, published after the war), 'but they at least obtained a nodding acquaintance with the work, a respect for tools, and an understanding of the need of timber for the war.'

To qualify for the Forestry Section of the WLA, members had to be over the age of twenty-one, a minimum that, in 1942, became the minimum enlistment age for the Women's Timber Corps. Members wore the same uniform as for the WLA, with the exception of the controversial hat - considered too cumbersome - a special green beret being substituted. The badge was also amended to show a fir tree, instead of the usual wheatsheaf, with the words 'Timber Corps, WLA' written around it. The crown, service, and devotion remained the same.

W. E. Shewell-Cooper advised any would-be recruits:

During the training period volunteers receive free board and lodging plus a personal allowance of 10s. per week. At the end of their course of training, volunteers are placed in employment in couples in a forest or sawmill at a starting wage of 45s. per week. Out of this the volunteers have to pay for their billets. The hours of work are from 7 a.m. to 4.30 p.m. with a half day off on Saturdays. Overtime must be worked if and when required.

Naturally it was not always like that! The price of a billet varied considerably, and the hours of work overlapped the statutory 4.30 p.m. The inability to administer the forestry workers was quickly apparent. Although the new Corps was recruited from the WLA, its administration was soon undertaken by the Home Timber Production Department of the Ministry of Supply in Bristol. Officers were appointed for Scotland, England and Wales, to deal with recruitment and training. Neither the WLA County Offices, nor their local representatives, took any responsibility for the welfare of the Timber Corps.

Whereas women could be sent on to farms with little or no training, some introduction to the work was an indispensable part of the WTC enrolment, or, at least, it was to begin with. As the war continued, training was to lose some of its importance, and, by February 1944, the training camps had been discontinued. In

Sorting acorns, at Parkend.
Members of the Women's Timber Corps sorting acorns at the Forestry Commission's training school at Parkend, in the Forest of Dean. Applicants numbered eighty a month in 1942, rising to one-hundred and eighty in early 1943.

1942, however, it was reasoned that there would be no Corps at all if the Government did not take note of safety. Observance of the safety rules had to become second nature to all timber workers. The regulations were there to be observed, and, for this reason, terms of employment and enrolment were, as they had been for the Women's Forestry Service of 1917, stricter than those for land workers.

Initial applicants, numbering eighty a month in April 1942 - a figure rising to one hundred and eighty by early 1943 - were catered for at the Commission's own school at Parkend, in the Forest of Dean, which was used for the training of measurers. Admission to the Corps came after vetting had taken place with the WLA County Secretaries, the Forestry Commission, and later the timber merchants. Those suited to active forestry work attended the Ministry of Labour camp at Culford, in Suffolk. Later, a training centre was established in a Royal Ordnance Factory Hostel at Wetherby, and smaller centres were opened in Wales and in Kent. In Scotland, where recruitment was higher - roughly one hundred and forty a month - training took place in two requisitioned country houses, near Brechin, and near Aberdeen.

Both the Parkend and Culford centres were disbanded during 1944, but for two years they taught students the business of forestry. After one month the qualified candidates were formally enrolled in the Timber Corps and sent to jobs up and down the country - usually a long way from home. Some went to work for timber merchants, while the majority were employed directly by the Home Timber Production Department. These jobs included felling; measuring; trimming and clearing; milling; selection for acquisition; pole selection; and all the negotiations for drawing up contracts of sale or purchase. These were jobs requiring a high level of intelligence and competence. In *Timber! Your Growing Investment*, the Commission declared:

> In 1919, there were only two commonly used sources of power in the woods
> - the muscles of a man and those of a horse. Machines were virtually
> unknown, and the only sounds to be heard in the forest, even at the busiest
> times, were the ring of the axe and the soft hiss of the hand cross-cut saw,
> followed by the crash of branches as a tall tree fell, and the horseman's cries
> as he urged a team of sturdy Shires or Clydesdales to drag a great log through
> the undergrowth.

It was only slightly more mechanised by the 1930s, and the writer might have added *women* as the source of power in both wars. What the Commission called 'the whirr of the power saw and the purr of the tractor' was still a novelty in some woodlands. Women learned to control the machinery and flex a few muscles, not in direct competition with the men, but very much on their own terms. But it was not all brawn; there were hours of boring, elementary, work to be undertaken in order to bring about the highly ambitious planting programmes:

> Hundreds of men, women and girls were engaged to carry out tedious
> repetitive tasks. Every spit of soil had to be turned by the spade, while every

seed was sown, and every seedling transplanted, entirely by hand. Even more troublesome was the weeding for every tiny seedling weed that threatened the small trees had to be removed with hand tools or a girl's nimble fingers.

The proximity of the Welsh coalfields to a source of pit props meant that WTC members were sent to isolated camps in what was, for most, a foreign land. In 1942, the Ministry of Supply in Bristol began to reorganise the Welsh Division. One half was to carry on with the management of the Commission's 60,000 acres of hill and forest, while the rest ceased practising forestry in any proper sense. Instead, it would buy up, fell, and convert timber, for the war effort - necessarily employing the WTC. George Ryle was involved in the discussions:

> Bristol produced a magnificent lady described ... as their Chief Woman Officer (CWO) and as soon as any of the divisions needed Timber Corps girls in sufficient numbers, she was able to produce Women's Welfare Officers to attend to all of their needs - lodging problems, the setting up of tin hut camps, homesick problems, rations, uniform, health, and especially boy-friend problems.

Members' welfare was one of the most difficult problems facing the Department, and the pressure on Officers was enormous. In England and Wales the members were widely scattered, and the establishment of camps or hostels could only be justified where no other accommodation was available. Some found a bed in Ministry of Supply hostels serving Royal Ordnance factories, but billets in the more remote villages, especially in Scotland, had to rely on often very primitive camps. Many women living in towns had come to take certain municipal services for granted. Many of the CWOs in particular expected slightly more in the way of comfort than they invariably found, and, in consequence, were often felt by prospective landladies to be demanding the impossible, given the circumstances of war.

Some concern was also expressed around the village of Treglog when, shortly after the Commission had taken possession of the nearby mansion of Bryn-cothi, an American army camp was discovered nearby. Concern was followed by a sigh of relief when the American camp was closed down. However, for the short time that the GIs and WTC lived in such close proximity, life was uneventful in the way of wartime romances, and when the Americans marched out they left behind them only welcome gifts of tinned foods and other rationed rarities; nothing else!

At Bryn-cothi the women could train in tractor driving; sawmill work, at a steam-engined mill beside the river; loading and pitwood preparation; timber measuring; record keeping and bookwork of all kinds. To accommodate them, the mansion was fitted with extra bathrooms (the WTC rules insisted on baths - but more often than not this was an impossibility), a kitchen range, and a large clothes-drying room: another luxury not afforded to every WTC member, nor indeed the majority of WLA members! The Ministry of Supply provided camp-beds and some basic furniture. The warden was to be selected by the CWO, and the Welfare Officer would oversee the arrival and establishment of the Corps members. Among the first group to occupy the converted mansion that first Thursday night was one 'Honourable', a clergyman's daughter, several factory and shop girls, colliers' daughters, and an artist. Once in uniform it was impossible to tell one from another; they became 'Bryn-cothi girls', and were involved in the operation which was to be responsible for cutting down very nearly a third of the measurable living trees in Britain, in the years between 1941-6.

Demand for the women's services from those in the timber trade was slow in coming. In both Wales and Scotland in particular there was a good deal of initial scepticism concerning the ability of women to operate sawmills and haul timber. The Commission was ready, willing, and able, to train and to use nearly all the applicants, but, predictably, it was only when the labour shortage became acute that the sawmill owners and private timber merchants took them on. By the time recruitment to the WTC closed and home timber production was reaching its peak, the response was such that demand far exceeded the supply, and, by December 1943, eight hundred and two women were employed privately in England, and one hundred and seventy-two in Scotland. Private employers were required to apply the Land Army conditions of service and the standard rate of pay.

Charcoal burning, c. 1943.
Many Timber Corps worked on the charcoal burners. Before burning, the wood had first to be cut, and then peeled - a tedious job which at this time had still to be done by hand.

The worry, expressed by the WFGA in 1938, that unskilled labour would dilute women's hard-won approval was, in the Timber Corps at least, solved to the women's advantage. The Forestry Commission was a specialist body, and its standard of training necessarily higher than that for the Land Girls. The business of forestry is more exacting than farm work - a fact that led eventually to a higher standard of achievement. Russell Meiggs, in *Home Timber Production*, wrote afterwards:

> There is no doubt that the Women's Timber Corps fulfilled the intention with which it was founded and made a significant contribution to the great production drive. It was no less true that many mistakes were made, and that better results could have been achieved. In the urgent pressure for increased production it was dangerously easy to sacrifice quality to quantity. In view of the testing nature of work in the woods it would have been wiser to have adopted a stiffer physical standard for membership of the Corps, but it is doubtful whether the Ministry of Labour would have looked with favour on large-scale rejections after a month of training.

Although recruitment to the WTC ended in July 1943, in the period that followed it was to consolidate its reputation. Welfare Officers were relieved at last of the everlasting task of finding suitable lodgings, and free instead to concentrate on what was fast becoming an élite team of women forestry workers. Special courses were held to provide leadership training, and over fifty members were promoted to foreman grade, taking charge of complete operations, controlling men as well as women. By 1944, the unfit - or those drawn to forestry as a 'soft option' - had left the Corps, leaving only those women who had training, experience, and the will to keep the job going efficiently. According to Russell Meiggs, even camp life improved:

> Camp life was enlivened by concert parties, film shows, classes and discussions, and it remained a feature of Scottish camps that unlike their pampered English sisters, who had no responsibilities for catering and paid a standard weekly charge, inmates should, with the help of a supervisor, plan their own meals and pay for what they chose to have.

In 1945, the Ministry of Supply asked their Assistant Medical Officer to review the health of the Corps. Some three hundred members were examined from camps and billets in England, Wales, and Scotland. She found no general deterioration in health, and was impressed by the general cheerfulness. Only among members with the longest service were there signs of undue fatigue, and absence due to gynaeco-logical causes was less than in most industries.

When, in August 1946, the WTC was disbanded it is not surprising that many, including key measurers, who had become essential to the effective maintenance of Commission operations, chose to stay on - some already married to other foresters.

114

9
Lumber Jills and Pole Cats!

Recollections of the Women's Timber Corps

Members have made their mark in every branch of the work, and have played a substantial part in the Victory of Production. It was expected that they would manage such work as measuring. It was not even surprising that some of them would be able to take on acquisition work, select trees for telegraph poles, and play an effective part in the census of standing timber. It has also been proved that, when the work is well organised, woman can fell light timber as neatly as men, drive and maintain heavy lorries and tractors, and even gain the respect of old hands on the saw benches.

Meet the Members, A Record of the Timber Corps of the WLA.

I wanted to work with trees because, having been brought up as a small child in London's East Ham, I had never seen trees, until at the age of five or so, a Sunday School outing found us at Epping Forest, where I ran off from the noisy fair into a clearing, and fell in love with the quiet trees.

When war came, I was taking School Certificate, and in 1940 got a job in a London office during the Battle of Britain. Our firm evacuated to Bristol just in time for the Blitz there! Young women of eighteen were being called up for the forces, and, in order to avoid factory work or the ATS, I volunteered to work with trees. I wanted to plant trees, so applied to the Forestry Commission, but there were no vacancies and I was advised to try the Ministry of Supply's newly-formed Women's Timber Corps, within the Home Grown Timber Production Department.

I was accepted for training at Bryn-cothi House in Abergorlech village, sixteen miles from Carmarthen, in South Wales. There were sixteen of us from all walks of life, but the place was like a barracks. Very primitive lavatories, no hot water ... but the villagers (especially the Chapel people) were very kind. Training included tree recognition in summer or winter, clearing brushwood, cutting light timber, measuring timber, and driving tractors or motorboats (for haulage across Scottish lochs later on). Girls were then segregated into the jobs they were considered most suitable for. I went on to train as a timber measurer.

This work [involved] the measuring of timber and counting of pit props, to gauge a man's earnings by piece-rates. Hard woods: oak, ash, elm, beech, sycamore - any trees which bore leaves - were paid at 2d. per cubic foot. Soft woods: all larch, firs, spruce, and pine - anything which bore needles - were paid at 1½d. per cubic foot. Each tree's number was scored on its base (not on the bark) with a scribing-knife: like a strong penknife with a sharp cutting hook on the end. The trees were entered into a notebook: first the number allocated, then the species of tree, the length and girth, and lastly the volume (which equalled the length times the girth). To find the girth, we measured half-way along the tree, then dropped the tape measure over the 'waist' of the tree. Then the narrow, curved steel measuring-sword was pushed under the tree, away from you. When the hook of the sword caught the square metal loop on the end of the tape, both ends of the tape were drawn together as though measuring the waist of someone lying on the ground. Volume was worked out in the evenings, with the help of a Ready Reckoner. The men were paid once a fortnight. The timber girl not only collected all measurements but worked out all wage sheets, and took wage packets round to the various woods each pay day, with hundreds of pounds in her haversack.

As each forest was cut down, the unit, including its measurer, would move on somewhere else, and I always had to find my own digs. [This was] sometimes very difficult in a strange town, especially when American soldiers were able to offer landladies much higher subsistence allowances. I also worked in sawmill offices, working on 'sawn' not 'round' timber. The workmen were sometimes resentful at first, not liking it that 'townees' were checking on work they had been doing for years. We had been warned, very strongly, that if we 'passed' timber props which did not qualify for the minimum measurements they might collapse and cause a miner's death. But when the men realised we were being fair they became more reasonable to us.

Our Christian names were never used. Neither was 'Miss Somebody-or-Other'. They always called us by the name of the place we came from. By now, my family had long-since moved from London, to Romford, in Essex - so 'Romford' I was called!

After the war, I trained as a teacher, and met my Welsh husband at our first school in Essex. So, on subsequent trips to South Wales to visit his parents, I have been able to visit friends I made during my time as a wartime Timber Girl.

Mrs Elsie Hughes, Stowmarket, Suffolk.

In 1940 I was offered a place in the WTC at forestry nurseries in Cowbridge, Glamorgan, where I stayed until May 1945, when I went to Oxfordshire. An aunt of mine had been a recruiting officer in the 1914 war, but I did not know this until after my enrolment in the WLA in September 1939 - so was in no way influenced. I just thought it would be a change from dressmaking!

For two years I was a foreman with a gang of girls, felling, measuring, clearing brushwood, and burning, etc. I was allowed to leave in May 1945 because I was expecting my first baby, and the work was rather strenuous for an expectant mother.

In the early days, after the nursery work, I was employed felling wood for the charcoal kilns; [the charcoal] was used in the making of gas masks. Later on, I took a course as a timber measurer at Parkend, in the Forest of Dean. There followed many different jobs and incidents, and those years were spent in various parts of mid- and south Wales, and almost a year in Hertfordshire. I remember we used to load the timber by tractor and tripod method. I can remember being bombed out of our billet in a lovely big house at Llandaff, on the outskirts of Cardiff. Land-mines were dropped and exploded a few days later, Llandaff Cathedral being a casualty. One of our number, a girl from Essex (where I came from), was transferred to the WLA, and was killed in a threshing-machine accident in Pembrokeshire.

In my spare time, I collected for National Savings, and there was a surprising amount of money hidden under mattresses, which I persuaded the men working in the sawmills to unearth and invest. I organised dances, with the help of a band from a local army camp, and also started a course of ballroom dancing in the village.

Mrs Gwendoline Porter, Wells, Somerset.

As a child, and, indeed until I left to join the Women's Timber Corps, I lived in the Forest of Dean. My mother's family were very much associated with forestry, so what other war work could I choose to do? The Forestry School, where young men were trained to be foresters, was actually in the village where I lived, but that was closed when all the residents left to go to war. Then suddenly, during 1942, lots of glamorous-looking females arrived to occupy the school, and train to be WTC girls. It was all very exciting for the village, especially when young men in reserved occupations arrived.

I was then in a partially reserved occupation, desperate to get away, so the wheels were set in motion. But, sadly, the courses at the school were then finished, and my friend and I were notified that we were to go to a place near Bury St Edmunds to train. We gaily set off from the village, breeches and all, mine quite three inches too big round the waist. Unfortunately, I did not keep a diary, but I remember we arrived at Bury St Edmunds, in Suffolk, where we met up with many other recruits. We were all taken by open lorry on a journey to a camp full of nissen huts, miles from anywhere. We were there for six weeks.

At the end of our training we were sent out in twos and threes to various places around the country. My destination turned out to be a timber-yard in Burton on Trent - not quite my idea of forestry! We did all sorts of things there, measuring, working on a small saw, cutting bungs for beer casks. [Then] I got a transfer back to the Forest of Dean, where they needed measurers, the thing I wanted to do.

Generally, life in the local communities was very good. I can't remember being rebuffed at all, and my living conditions were good at Burton on Trent. On my return to the Forest of Dean I was able to live at home, so one could say I was fortunate. I very much enjoyed my WTC days.

Sheila McIntyre, Chichester, Sussex.

At the outbreak of war I was in a reserved occupation: comptometer operator/wages clerk at a colliery in Wallsend-on-Tyne, Northumberland (where I was born). One day I was reading a magazine, and was impressed with details of the WLA doing timber work, especially timber measuring. I applied to the office of the Home Grown Timber Production Department, where I sat a test. The last sum was calculating cubic capacity, which I managed. Girls had also to be of secondary education, which limited the number of applicants.

I was issued with WLA uniform, and my first posting was to Pickering, in North Yorkshire. A freckled-faced boy called 'Ginger' Benson met me at the station to take me to my digs, a lovely modern house on the outskirts of a market town situated five miles up the Pickering-to-Whitby line. The foreman had advised that the new recruit must have a bicycle, and as I did not possess one, nor could ride one, I had to walk in new heavy shoes along a railway track. My feet were so swollen I could not walk home in my shoes. I recall there were two or three railway workers cottages by the sawmill, and Mrs Eddy, who befriended me, later let me use her parlour to eat my lunch in, and gave me goats milk to drink. She loaned me a pair of rubber overshoes, and I had to slop home in these. Needless to say, I could not go to work for a few days: my heels were raw, and bleeding. My landlady put me into a warm bath, and I wept, wondering why I had left Wallsend and joined the WLA.

My landlady had a bicycle, and gave me lessons around the avenue, but I just could not ride. However, I did make friends with Dorothy, who lived with her parents in the same avenue. She worked as a Land Girl, tomato-growing, with a large nursery, where she had already worked before it had had to change to food production. My problem of walking to work along the railway track was finally solved by finding a small bus taking timber workers to another operation. I was able to travel to a certain point, and walk down the wooded slopes to the saw mill.

I was happy in Pickering, but after a while my lift stopped when the operation finished. I was transferred to Haltwhistle, in Northumberland; the beginning of the South Tyne Valley. I was much busier at a larger mill. I did the invoices, wages, and consignment notes in a log cabin office set away from the mill. The workmen were mostly unskilled men, and it was sad to learn that they had had long stretches of unemployment. Haltwhistle had been on a par with Jarrow during the depression years.

I shared digs with another timber measurer in the lodge of Ballister Castle. For 25s. per week I was well cared for, and once again made life-long friends. A lorry used to take us all to work, and was also used to take timber to be despatched from

118

Featherstone station, near Featherstone Castle, where, later, high ranking German officers were kept as prisoners of war.

I recall the cold winter mornings when the ink would be frozen in the inkwell; and deer coming down to the cabin, and robins sharing my crumbs. My worst memory is of a serious accident. I was always reporting to my foreman that his first aid box lacked a tourniquet. It happened that two brothers were given a rare piece-rate job to quarter props. Bill was over-anxious to earn a few more shillings, and in haste caught the circular saw - cutting the inside of his upper right arm to the bone. I ran to the Operations office, in the same clearing, demanded their tourniquet, and ran back. Bill, nearly drained of blood, was taken to the nearest hospital in Haltwhistle, then transferred to Hexham, where a young Australian saved his arm. But he could never work again. Bill always used to say I was the girl who saved his life, as the Matron had said he could only have lived another few minutes. It was only later that night when I really thought about it; I was really scared, and wished my mother was with me. Safety regulations had to be very, very strict, and one got used to the screaming of the saws. I loved the smell of the sawdust.

Anne Mannion, Richmond, North Yorkshire.

I served in the Women's Timber Corps from 1942 until December 1946, when I was transferred to the Forestry Commission in Coed-y Brenin Forest, where I worked as a Forest Clerk until 1956. I was probably one of the first Forest Clerks in the Commission.

In the first months of 1942 we did cross-cutting (timber and pitprops), peeled wood wool, burnt brash. Some of us did extraction with horses, and one particular lady from Lancashire handled this TD6 better than any man, and on extremely dangerous slopes. When I joined I expected to be moved to Scotland, or South Wales, but I only moved eighteen miles away from my home village of Llanuwchi-lyn, near Bala. One day, soon after joining, I objected to the fact that on cross-cutting we girls had less per 100 lineal foot than the men and told our boss that it was very unfair and sex-discriminating. The answer to my complaint came with my transfer eighteen miles away, as Forest Measurer for four timber-fellers. I was eighteen at the time. Later I went to the office to work, and married one of the four timber-fellers!

I worked with all sorts of people. Irishmen galore. Displaced persons joined us, too, including one Hungarian, who ate swedes, apples, and chunks of bread at work, and only drank water. I think he had been wanted by the Gestapo, and he would never have his photograph taken.

It is a fact that once you have worked in timber you always feel an affinity with trees, which you never lose. My husband and I have passed this love to our boys, too, as did my father to me.

Cassie Jones, Llanfachneth, Gwynedd.

By this personal message I wish to express to you

Ada Mary Nash

my appreciation of your loyal and devoted service
as a member of the Women's Land Army from
5th January, 1942   to   30th November, 1950
Your unsparing efforts at a time when the victory
of our cause depended on the utmost use of the
resources of our land have earned for you the
country's gratitude.

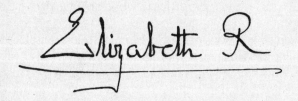

The release certificate presented to a WLA member in November 1950.

10
Disbanding

VISCOUNTESS ASTOR Plymouth, Sutton, U. - Is it not true that the W.L.A. are underpaid, overworked and very often badly housed, and will not the Prime Minister in the largeness of his heart consider that? (Cheers)
MR. CHURCHILL - That is one of the sweeping generalisations which we have come to regard as characteristic of the noble lady (Laughter). I should hesitate to draw any deductions therefrom. I am of the opinion that the House should have an opportunity to debate this matter, but it is for the Leader of the House to say what is the most convenient way of fitting it in with the already crowded programme of Government business.

The Times, 9 March, 1945

Although often referred to as the 'Cinderella Service', the story of the WLA was not to have a fairy-tale ending. Its members were asked to stay at their posts, long after August 1945, knowing that they were not to be included in the Reinstatement of Civil Employment Act. By her criticism of bureaucracy Lady Denman had made enemies as well as friends. She had used very straightforward negotiations in 1938 to get her way over the establishment of an organised Land Army. In 1941 she succeeded in freeing the WLA from the Ministry of Agriculture, to operate instead as a 'semi-independent Unit Organisation'; she had alienated members of the WFGA; and was seen by some to have favoured the WIs in administrative roles, thus retaining rural authority and power in the same hands as it had always been. The fact that she had more than 'got the job done' was insufficient to counter charges of autocracy.

As the tide of war shifted in favour of the Allies, the Government was increasingly looking for ways to save money. In August 1943, when the strength of the WLA in England and Wales stood at 72,408 volunteers, the War Cabinet ordered an end to recruitment. Although by the end of that year the total membership had reached 80,000 [there had been a maximum of 23,000 in the First World War] women land workers were thenceforward to be supplemented by Italian prisoners of war, and also by 'paying guests'. As Angus Calder explains in *The People's War*.

> By July 1943, there were nearly forty thousand Italian prisoners of war at
> work in the fields, many of them billeted with farmers. Soldiers stationed at
> home, and even GIs, also turned out to help with the harvest; and the general
> public discovered that farm work was a dignified, and notably cheap, way
> of taking a holiday in wartime.

These additional volunteers were charged for accommodation, but their wages
usually covered the costs. Cycling members of the two hundred or so weekend clubs
returned to their homes on Sunday nights exhausted, but with hearts full of patriotic
satisfaction. The arrival of these newcomers, 'doing their bit', in the countryside
began to undermine the position of WLA members. Farmers, eager to save money
where they could, saw the merit in a transient work-force, as against paying a full-
time Land Girl who might also be billeted on the farmhouse. The gradual increase
in wages contributed to the argument. In March 1941, the minimum wage for
farmworkers had been fixed at 32s. for a working week of up to forty-eight hours,
with overtime pay. For the Land Girl, billeted on the farm, there was a statutory
wage of 16s. a week, with paid overtime for work in excess of forty-eight hours; she
also paid her share of a National Health and Unemployment Insurance stamp
herself.

On 3 January 1944, recruiting for the WLA started again, although now any
woman wishing to join had to obtain permission from her Employment Exchange.
Certainly the other women's services, WRNS, ATS, and WAAFS, offered a more
secure future and considerably more kudos than the WLA. At this crucial stage of
recruitment it would have made more sense for the Ministry of Labour to have
offered some inducement to women to remain on the land rather than raise new
recruits. The training and experience acquired by the existing Land Girls was
wasted if they left the service, and some encouragement to those prepared to take
on the job of a farm labourer would have been welcomed. Unfortunately, the
opportunity was not taken.

By March 1944, the Government had decided that although women were still
able to enlist, the size of the Land Army should be limited. Obviously the bonus of
unexpected workers - the weekend cyclists and youth groups - added weight to
objections concerning labour allocation.

Between 1940 and 1943, such discussions, or arguments, over labour had been
a secondary topic of conversation as members of the War Agricultural Committee's
were instructed to carry out a 'Domesday' survey of British agriculture. In the
September 1940, issue of *The Land Girl*, Inez Jenkins encouraged pride in the first
three letters of the alphabet:

> In each county the War Agricultural Executive Committee is now carrying
> out a survey of farms. Every farm will be classified as A, as B, or as C . . .
> the C farms are the bad farms and there, unless the farmer can mend his ways

- and quickly - the farm will be taken over and farmed by the War Agricultural Executive Committee itself . . . where in the alphabet are you?

Only rarely, however, were Land Army members able to influence the placing of their particular farm in the scale of excellence, although early in 1945 there was news of a group of WLA girls who had succeeded in up-grading a herd of Shorthorns at the War Ag's farm at Sutton Hoo, in Suffolk. As E. Mary Ball wrote in *Farmer and Stock-Breeder:*

When the Committee first bought the herd a cowman was put in charge; when he left, five girls took over under a 23-year old forewoman, Miss Maxine Lewis. This meant that some 50 head of stock was under direct supervision by WLA personnel, and its members were responsible to the Committee for the welfare of the whole herd.

Miss Lewis, her assistant, two stock girls, and a carter, formed a self-contained unit doing all the feeding, machine milking, bookkeeping, and record keeping - even grooming and exercising the pedigree Shorthorn bull used for grading-up, as well as looking after calving animals. During 1944 the River Deben burst its banks and flooded well over three-quarters of the farm's pasture land, but the girls dealt with all that and more. To counter any arguments about over-staffing, Miss Ball argued:

It must be remembered that these girls are producing most of the food for the animals, utilising very poor soil, which was never very productive, and by their good management and handling are grading-up a herd which will produce TT milk and be of considerable value in a short while. Added to which they have a good team spirit, work 9½ hours a day, seven days a week. with free week-ends by arrangement with each other.

By the end of 1943, the War Ags had completed their survey, classifying farms in terms of production, soil type, and state of repair. During the three years of their investigations nearly 400,000 acres were taken over by the War Ags themselves. Official repossession of land, or the implementation of an order to plough, was never a welcome move from anyone's point of view. Many Land Girls found themselves with a change of boss practically overnight. A correspondent to *Country Life*, in August 1941, recounts one of the many incidents he had come across:

A truculent woman farmer flatly refused to plough, defied a compulsory Order, and, when a contractor was sent to break up the pasture scheduled, fastened up the gate with a cow chain. The lock was picked and ploughing started, whereupon the lady stood in the path of the tractor and said (literally) 'Over my dead body'. The driver stopped, but the District Officer, infuriated by the whole silly business, said to the driver, 'Get down and let me drive'. Convinced that a District Officer was quite capable of driving over her dead body, the lady went home - checked, but far from defeated. Her next move was to release a very irascible Friesian bull, but the tractor driver saw it coming, unhitched the plough, and drove straight for the bull, which turned and fled. The joy of the chase was too much for the driver, for he continued to pursue the bull to the end of a long field bounded by a quickset hedge. The bull plunged through it - and the lady gave in!

Although members of the WLA and WTC received no service medals or decorations, they were eligible for recognition of acts of bravery in the same way as other civilians.

One of the first members to be honoured was Miss E. Margaret Smyth, Organising Secretary for East Kent, who was awarded the MBE. Miss Smyth had given 'untiring efforts' to Land Girls working in the dangerous areas of East Kent, throughout weeks of intensive bombing, when many houses were damaged or destroyed. Her coolness, courage, and devotion to duty, was especially noted.

In May, 1942, *The Times* noted the award of a BEM to Mrs Kathleen Mitchell, a farmer's wife, and Miss Grace Harrison, a farm worker and tractor driver of the Women's Land Army. They were said to have made an unexampled effort, and shown sustained bravery and devotion to duty, in carrying on with their farming under gunfire, and attacks from the enemy:

> The farm is at the nearest point to the Continent and is scarred with filled-in shell holes. The farm buildings are probably the most vulnerable in the country, yet work was carried on throughout the Battle of Britain and ever since. Mr and Mrs Mitchell, with the help of Miss Harrison, remained at the farm and not only saved their own crops but also those of other farms which had been evacuated.

Vita Sackville-West recorded the Mitchell's example in some detail in *The Women's Land Army*, quoting the remark by Grace Harrison that 'the war is only a sideshow after all. The real show is the farm.'

There was also mention of an ex-librarian, who was awarded a War Agricultural Committee badge for courage at her post, on a lonely farm near Dover, after coming under shelling, bombing, and machine-gunning three times by an enemy aircraft.

At the end of April 1944, WLA Headquarters staff were moved back to London. Whose decision this was, or why it was taken, remains a mystery. Possibly someone wished to loosen Lady Denman's grip on the WLA by removing it from her private home. The personal relationship between the Honourable Director and Robert Hudson, the Minister of Agriculture, was at least cordial. Less so, was that between Lady Denman and the Government. No sooner, however, had the return of the WLA to London been contrived, than the 'doodlebug' V1 bombing began, and Lady Denman was asked to reopen Balcombe.

The WLA Headquarters returned to the Sussex countryside; but the spirit of the Land Army had taken a battering, and though still resiliant, its members continued to attract ridicule from the Press, and from the other womens' services. They were also finding it more difficult to obtain secure jobs, and many were simply tired. The upheaval of the administration's move from Balcombe to London, and then back again, put a strain on the good humour of the long-suffering staff. It had again become clear that the WLA, as far as the Government was concerned, was paying the price of its independence. Removing the WLA from the direct control of the Ministry of Agriculture in 1941 had been a bold move. The present Lord Denman, who remembers his aunt as a truly remarkable woman, believes that in getting the whole thing run from her own home 'she beat the civil servants in one stroke'. The essential difference in the running of the WLA from the spring of 1941, was, according to Gervas Huxley, that Lady Denman:

> was empowered to make all day-to-day administrative decisions, as well as appointments and promotions. She could also incur expenditure on uni-forms, propaganda, etc. within a fixed annual sum of money.

By 1944, the practical running of the WLA was the least of Lady Denman's worries. She had loyal, competent helpers, and a workforce of willing volunteers who had weathered the storms of both unfriendly (and friendly!) farmers, and had succeeded in proving their capabilities and staying power. The problems lay neither in the past, nor in the present, but in the future.

In the spring of 1942, Lady Denman had learned from the Ministry of Agriculture that WLA personnel were to be excluded from any scheme that might be adopted by the inter-departmental Committee on the 'Further Education of Demobilized Members of HM Forces and Civil Defence Services'. Her immediate reaction, Gervas Huxley records was that she found it strange 'that any Committee could think it reasonable that a civilian nurse should be eligible for training as a veterinary surgeon but that a member of the Women's Land Army should be debarred from this advantage.'

Committees had been appointed to ponder the best strategy for the post-war period. Once the war ended, it was planned to offer those men and women who had joined the armed forces, or the auxiliary services, minor rewards to assist with resettlement. Since these were intended to embrace a wide section of wartime organisations it would have been reasonable to suppose that they might also include the enormous 'army' of women which had volunteered to keep the nation fed. This proved not to be the case, and if there was any thought that argument alone might remedy the situation it became very clear from Committee discussions, which continued into 1943, and then into 1944, that the decision to exclude the Land Army from such benefits was becoming entrenched.

In 1944, despite the advocacy of the Minister of Agriculture, it was further decreed that Land Girls should receive no clothing coupons or grants when they were demobilised. Any woman land worker who ventured into one of the Resettlement Advice offices was soon disabused of the notion that she would obtain the equivalent of a male 'demob suit' in either coupons or cash. She was to receive no post-war benefits, nor any of the privileges, however insignificant, accorded to the other Women's Services. By November 1944, Lady Denman had decided that her resignation was the only weapon left to her in the fight for better post-war benefits. Accordingly, she wrote to Robert Hudson. In January 1945, she was informed by the Permanent Head of the Ministry that the Government's intentions remained unchanged. Still hoping to influence the War Cabinet's mind, Lady Denman continued to lobby strongly against these considered injustices, pointing out the essential work of the Land Army.

On the 15 February 1945, the Right Honourable Ernest Bevin, Minister of Labour, informed the House of Commons that:

> Persons who have had full-time paid service in the armed forces and auxiliary services, the Merchant Navy, or Civil Defence, and were previously in business or work on their own account, will be eligible for a grant up to a maximum of £150 where this is necessary to supplement their own resources and enable them to restart.

Resettlement grants would, in consequence, be extended to Civil Defence and other auxiliary workers, but still not include the WLA. Bevin's reason, or perhaps excuse, was that the WLA came under the jurisdiction of the Ministry of Agriculture. Knowing, as he did, the conditions under which Lady Denman had engineered the removal of the Women's Land Army from the control of his own Ministry, he would have known that the Ministry of Agriculture had made no extra provision whatsoever for the resettlement of Land Army volunteers. Robert Hudson might, in turn, have argued that his Ministry assumed that such matters should have been dealt with at War Cabinet level. In the event, Lady Denman's resignation, as Honorary Director of the Women's Land Army for England and Wales, reached the Minister of Agriculture on the very day that the Resettlement terms were announced. Copies of her letter were released to the Press, and *The Times* carried almost the full text on the 20 February:

> The Land Army is a uniformed service recruited on a national basis by a government department, and the work which its members have undertaken, often at considerable financial sacrifice, is in my view as arduous and exacting as any branch of women's war work, and of as great importance to this country. Yet they have been refused post-war benefits and privileges accorded to such other uniformed and nationally organised services as the WRNS, the ATS, the WAAF, the Civil Nursing Reserve, the Police Auxiliaries, and the Civil Defence Services.
>
> This position is a serious one for Land Army members who will have as great a need as those in other services of Government assistance in the

problems of resettlement. As you know, I have protested against the omission of the Land Army from various Government schemes and also against the decision, now announced, that capital grants to assist in restarting business enterprises will be available after the war to men and women who have served whole time in the forces, the Merchant Navy, in the Civil Defence Services, but not to members of the Women's Land Army. It is this latest decision which has led me to feel that I must resign my present appointment, and that I can no longer appear to be responsible for a policy with which I do not concur.

The same issue carried three letters to the Editor all decrying the Government's decision. The argument continued in both the Press and in the Cabinet for some days. Those who complained, expressed their absolute dissatisfaction with the policy, although in the week following Lady Denman's resignation, Mr L. H. Newton declared himself an ally of the Minister of Labour by querying, again in *The Times*, the rights of the WLA over those of munition workers.

Almost every newspaper in the land carried the news of Lady Denman's resignation. The *Yorkshire Observer* headlined the story, 'A Mean Injustice'; the *Daily Mail* sported a cartoon by Neb, with the caption 'I suppose they think that communing with Nature for five years has been sufficient reward in itself'; while both the *News Chronicle* and *Sunday Express* continued to set out the arguments for and against the resettlement issue.

At the end of February, the Minister of Agriculture announced, mysteriously, that he had 'a special plan' for the WLA. In early March, the Prime Minister informed the House of Commons of the decision that had been reached concerning the extension of war gratuities. There was no mention of any special plan. On the contrary, Mr Churchill anticipated the disappointment which would be felt at the 'impossibility of extending concessions beyond those already indicated, without opening the doors to an unending succession of new and extended claims which could not be differentiated on any logical basis', although who might make such claims was never clarified. That same month, Lady Denman sent a two-page circular to all MPs, entitled 'The Land Army's Case for Post-War Benefit'. Almost all who replied to it pledged their support, and promised to do what they could to win over the Cabinet. The Executive Committee of the Liberal Party unanimously passed a resolution in support of Lady Denman, and the National Farmers' Union added its voice to the protest, saying that the decision was causing ill-feeling throughout the farming community.

In retrospect, the only way in which things might have been different would have been for the Land Girls and Timber Corps members to have been employed, and therefore directly paid, by the Government. This would have been difficult, if not impossible. Bureaucracy would have faced insuperable problems in coping with the immediacy of farming's needs, and any attempt to regiment such a scattered 'army' would surely have ended in chaos, and then neither the WLA nor the WTC would ever have achieved their respective purpose. The reasons for a separate administration were precisely those which argued against direct government control. In 1938, it had been very easy for the Government to agree to Lady Denman's generous offer to mastermind the entire operation, when the advantages of such an arrangement were obvious. It is to be doubted whether, at that point it occurred to anyone to query what the potential status of the Land Army might be when peace returned. The editorial in the April issue of *The Land Girl* was not concerned with history, and reflected justifiable outrage:

> The Government's pronouncement that the WLA would be excluded from all post-war financial benefits granted to other war Services was received with strong protest throughout the country. Nearly 200 Members of Parliament have signed their names in support of one or other of the three Motions put down by Mrs Cazalet Keir, Mrs Mavis Tate and Sir George Courthope. The Prime Minister has been asked to receive a deputation of Members representing all three political parties and there is to be a debate in the House of Commons.

Home and Country was perhaps a little less outraged, concentrating instead on the advantages:

> It is proverbially an ill wind that blows nobody good, and the loss sustained by the WLA through the resignation of Lady Denman from her Honorary Directorship is definitely the gain of the NFWI, who welcome her back and who hope to see very much more of her at Headquarters during 1945.

The practical Mrs Pyke speculated as to what would happen should the debate fail to move the Government. The natural impulse might be for members to 'throw down spades and ploughs, pens and typewriters', but such action, of course, could not be recommended. 'If the rest of us went,' she wrote, 'the Government would not suffer but the country would. It would be the people we have helped to feed, and the babies for whom we have helped to produce milk, who would go short.'

There was also the ever-increasing danger of food shortages to contend with. Germany's surrender would throw the responsibility for feeding Europe on the Allies, while at home, once demobilisation gathered pace, millions of former servicemen and women would need to be fed.

'The nation is still at war,' readers of *The Land Girl* were reminded, 'the food situation has never been more difficult and farming has never faced the prospect of a more acute shortage of labour. Clearly the Land Army must find its second wind.'

Some, putting their faith in the adage that 'while there's life there's hope' felt a continuing dedication to duty might influence official attitudes in the case of resettlement claims. It would anyway have been unthinkable for members of the WLA to have 'downed tools'. Such action would, quite properly, have engendered critical public reaction and damaged the justifiable pride that members had in their war record. Nor should it be forgotten that, at the same time, there was an equally dedicated and completely overlooked 'army' of women working on the land - farmers' wives and daughters - who pointed out that they had neither expected, nor received, payment for their role in home food production. There was also an existing body of male farm workers, who knew that this was no time to quit. Indeed, all men and women on the land responded instinctively to the truth behind Robert Hudson's appeal, in the summer of 1945, for 200,000 adults for harvest camps. 'Quite definitely', he said, 'the scale of rations next winter will depend largely on what we manage to gather in this summer and autumn.'

In spite of the one hundred and thirty-five MPs who tabled a question to the Prime Minister asking for further representations in respect of the WLA, Mr Churchill was adamant. He told the House that he would not embark on a competition for winning popularity by giving in to demands for grants. He must, he said, have due regard to the public and financial condition, '... nothing would be easier and, if I were base enough, more tempting, than to offer large and unconsidered concessions at the public expense'.

At last, on 16 May 1945, the Minister of Agriculture was able to announce some embarrassingly inadequate concessions. Members of the Land Army were to receive some help towards post-war training in line with that given to Civil Defence and Auxiliary war workers, and there was to be a grant of £150,000 to the WLA Benevolent Fund. The third and final concession caused some merriment, at least among the ranks. Members were to be allowed to keep their shoes, greatcoats (provided these were dyed navy blue), and, in some cases, their blouse - where one had been allocated. As *The Times* remarked, 'If, when they leave the WLA they have only this scanty attire, they will certainly need assistance from the Benevolent Fund.'

All over England and Wales, Land Girls posed for snap shots, holding a shoe in each hand, donned only in their coats and little else! Remembering her disappointment at the time, one woman wrote:

Although in 1940 the WLA was advertised as one of the Women's Services ... we were not entitled to Demobilisation grants as given to the other Services because we came under the auspices of the Ministry of Ag. & Fish. I wondered how the Services, and everyone else, would have survived without the farmers and their workers. A point politicans always seem to overlook as soon as peace is restored.

The same woman expressed some doubts over the saleability of a large number of ex-WLA jerseys - even through the usual recycling channels of Army Surplus Stores:

The jerseys weren't just used for keeping warm, and a lot I saw were stained with all sorts of unmentionables besides being very smelly. Some girls were particular about how they treated their work clothes but most were not, and when they got torn used very primitive methods of darning!

In October 1945, following the election of the Labour government, Tom Williams, the new Minister of Agriculture, presented the House of Commons with details of the release of those WLA members who had undertaken to serve for the duration of the war. Any woman who undertook to remain in the Land Army for another year would receive an extra week's holiday 'at the State's expense', with an extra three days for each additional year of service. Unfortunately, this applied only to women who had already served for two years, and left hundreds of women feeling rather hard-done by.

Although the Land Girls were disregarded by their government, their Patron, at least, never let them down. Indeed, the support of the King and Queen did a great deal to lift the declining morale of both staff and WLA members in the years leading up to 1950.

It was in 1941, shortly after the WLA had been freed from the control of the Ministry of Agriculture, that Lady Denman had approached the Queen, asking her to become Patron of the WLA. Royal patronage for women's land work was not a new idea. Queen Mary had interested herself in the running of Swanley, and in women's land work generally, and had given approval for her daughter, Princess Mary (who herself became Patron of the National Association of Landswomen), to take part in the 1919 farewell ceremony for the first Women's Land Army.

On accepting the invitation to become Patron of the WLA, Queen Elizabeth sent her portrait to the London recruiting office for display, and kept in touch with the Land Army. The Queen had previously shown her interest in, and support for, the Land Army by attending a party held at the Goldsmiths' Hall, on 14 March 1940, for two hundred and fifty Land Girls from England and Wales. Received by Lady Denman and Mr Arthur Wakely, Prime Warden of the Goldsmiths' Company, the Queen had inspected the four lines of Land Girls assembled in the Livery Hall. *The Times* duly reported the event:

> Instead of the distinguished and dignified guests of most City occasions, there were these farm girls in their attractive working kit of corduroy breeches, open-neck blouses, and green pullovers, and with the rosy cheeks of open-air workers ... the soft light of candles, flickering high up in three magnificent candelabra, illuminated a pleasing picture in which a large bouquet composed not merely of lilies and various spring blooms, but of cauliflower, carrots, tomatoes, and other fruits of the earth was a decorative reminder that harvest will come to reward good work on the land.

The Worshipful Company of Goldsmiths commemorated the occasion by presenting the Land Army with a silver fruit bowl, designed by Cyril James Shiner, which was 'to be competed for by members'. The bowl was returned to the Company by Lady Denman at the end of the war.

Land Girls were to be invited to the Palace on several occasions. On 3 July 1943, the Queen, accompanied by Princess Elizabeth and Princess Margaret, gave a party for 300 girls from all parts of the country. The surprise party was a fourth birthday celebration for the WLA. *The Times* noted that the girls 'were told only last week that they had been chosen to go to London for a special occasion, but until midday on Saturday they had no idea it was to be a party at Buckingham Palace.'

The party was at first due to be given in the gardens of the Palace, but the Queen decided that the Land Girls would have seen quite enough of gardens and was sure that the inside of the Palace would interest them more - particularly as rain threatened. Phyllis Cunningham was one of those who remembers the thoughtfulness of the Queen:

I was asked to represent the Isle of Ely at [the] Garden Party given for the WLA by Queen Elizabeth. Needless to say it was a great day, even though it rained. I knew then what it felt like to 'walk on air'. We had to wait in a long gallery full of Royal portraits before being ushered into the room where we found Queen Elizabeth and the two little Princesses awaiting us. After being presented, and shaking hands, I followed others into the room where we were given cucumber and paste sandwiches, and Dundee cake. Tea was poured from a delightful tea pot which had a strainer attached by little chains fixed each side of the spout. After tea, the Queen and the Princesses moved amongst the guests chatting, and the Queen told me she had been to the Isle of Ely only a short time before. She had pretty dark hair, and kind, dark blue eyes. I remember wondering wildly if she was accustomed to conversing with idiots gibbering with nerves! I still have my invitation card.

As my landlady had jeered 'I bet they give you bread and jam for tea' I secreted a paste sandwich in a pocket to take back to her to prove her wrong. She gave it to the cat!

A number of Land Girls had found employment on the Sandringham Estate in Norfolk, both on the farm, and in the woods, where they felled timber and lifted 40,000 young trees for the plantations and 50,000 for the nurseries.

On the Saturday of the Palace Garden party, the Duchess of Gloucester presented awards for good service at a Women's Land Army rally in Cambridge. Nearly 300 members of the Land Army from Huntingdonshire, Cambridgeshire, and the Isle of Ely, marched through the town, and later attended a meeting in the Guildhall for the awards ceremony. Huntingdon was also honoured by Queen Marie of Yugloslavia, who, accompanied by Lady Shepherdson, inspected a gathering of assorted Land Girls assembled from the farms around the Huntingdon WLA Headquarters.

By the end of 1945, it became clear that no part of the Resettlement Grant programme would be reversed. The shoes, greatcoats, and Benevolent Fund donation were to be the final concessions. The decision having been made, and accepted by the women volunteers, the Minister of Agriculture showed some degree of courage by announcing, on the 26 January 1948, that the Land Army,

Queen Marie of Yugoslavia *(centre picture)*, accompanied by Lady Shepherdson, inspecting a contingent of the Huntingdonshire WLA, c. 1944.

which still had an enrolled strength of 25,643 members, was to be asked to continue for another two or three years. A new agricultural expansion programme was planned and the women were needed to ensure its success. Although changes were to be made in the administration, WLA conditions of service would remain virtually the same. Any problems that might arise for the remaining Land Girls would have to be referred to the new Welfare Committees being set up to replace the Land Army County Committees. Where the Welfare Committees were unable, or unwilling, to help there was only one alternative, and that was an application to the WLA Benevolent Fund.

The Benevolent Fund
The Women's Land Army Benevolent Fund was registered under the War Charities Act in 1942. The various fund-raising events, previously held for the Spitfire Fund, could now be channelled into a Fund much closer to home. Its original function was to help volunteers who met with illness or accident, and who were not covered by other forms of help, and to assist with grants or loans for those women intending to remain on the land after the war ended. At first it was thought that the Fund - started by Lady Denman (who became its Chairman) - would have a secondary role to that of the Government's resettlement programme. In the event, it was to become essential for many women returning to pre-war occupations, or hoping to find new

employment. Even those, however, like Miss M. V. Brett, who was involved in setting up the Fund, never envisaged it lasting as long as it did. Miss Brett continued to serve in the Fund's administration until it was finally wound up in 1981.

Contributions to the Fund came from all quarters, including the Ford Motor Company; Fisons of Ipswich; ICI; Messrs Huntley & Palmer; Cadburys; Ransomes; R & W Paul; Josephs Aluminium Works; Produce Canners; George Gray; and Parker Shoes. In May 1943, the King himself sent a donation, and the Queen agreed to become the Fund's Patron. Profits from the sale of Vita Sackville-West's *The Women's Land Army* went into the Fund coffers, as did those from the sales of the Timber Corps' *Meet the Members.* Contributions from Land Army members themselves poured in from every county, sometimes from individuals, but more often the result of some local fund-raising event. During 1946 a series of pictorial county maps were sold in aid of the Fund, the first of their kind to be published since 1688!

Regular news of the various fund-raising events was reported in *The Land Girl*, just as those for the Spitfire Fund had been. Members were informed as to how, and upon what, the money was spent - as in this extract from a copy of *The Land Girl*, in April 1945:

> During the first three months of 1945, 715 grants for varying sums have been made from the Benevolent Fund to a total of £4,292. For the same period in 1944 the number of grants was 328, and in 1943 only 30 ... The great majority of grants have been to help in cases of financial hardship caused through illness. Assistance has also been given towards dental and optical expenses, ambulances, surgical appliances, Rest Break fees, special treatment, and fares to hospital - to mention only some of the ways in which the Fund has helped.

In February 1948, *Land Army News*, successor to *The Land Girl*, gave another update on expenditure:

> Convalescing after an illness very often means long, dull days with practically nothing to amuse you. The Benevolent Fund has, among its many cases, two ex-Land Girls who have been ill for about two years. The Fund has been helping them with their expenses and their health has improved considerably, but they are still unable to go to work. So, these enterprising girls have been making the most delightful soft toys and plastic bags in their own homes, and at Christmas time earned quite a lot of money. They hope to develop a regular business and work this up as their health improves. In order to give them a start, the Benevolent Fund Committee has now helped each girl to buy a sewing machine and hopes it will not be long before their trade is flourishing.

It was never the intention of the Fund to help with the purchase of houses or furniture, or with mortgage repayments, nor was it able to offer loans. The Chairman of the WLA Committee for the London and Middlesex Area, Mrs M. R. Beale, OBE, a long-standing Chairman of the Fund, *was* empowered to help with debts, at her discretion, although this depended upon how the debts arose. The main aim of the Fund was to help members and, later on, ex-members, who found themselves in straitened financial circumstances as a direct result of their Land Army duties, particularly during illness or long periods of unemployment. Initially it was administered by Committees which included the Chief Officers of the Women's Timber Corps. After 1950, applications were considered by a Grants Committee which met once a fortnight. Miss Brett, the Fund Secretary, remembers that from the time the WLA was disbanded, and until 1981, they:

> had an arrangement with the Department of Employment and the Department of Health and Social Security whereby every two years during the winter a poster about the Fund [was] displayed in every Labour Exchange and Social Security office in England and Wales. This brought the existence of the Fund to the notice of ex-members who were either out of work or ill, and was the means of bringing us a great many cases. All Medical Social Workers in hospital were kept informed about our work, and also Citizen's Advice Bureaux. Various social work organisations, such as the Red Cross, also brought cases to our notice.

Between 1942 and 1980, 32,624 grants were made, many of them to women who had no certain direction once their days as a WLA volunteer ended. The Benevolent Fund also offered Homecraft Courses which were intended to help any member or ex-member who wished to start married life with confidence, having missed out on 'the example of their respective mothers due to Land Army service'. A new centre was opened in April 1946, near Melton Mowbray, following the successful establishment of Cromwell's Cottage, at Whepstead, in Suffolk.

The surviving WLA continued to provide women farm labour until it was disbanded. The Queen presided over the final parade for five hundred members of the WLA held at Buckingham Palace, on the morning of 21 October 1950, before going on to attend the christening of her granddaughter, Princess Anne, in the afternoon. The band of the Irish Guards led the march into the Palace. In the words of *The Times* report:

> Her Majesty inspected long-service badges, and said that a farewell was always an occasion of some sadness and their sadness could be lightened by the pride in their achievements. She had been their patron for the past nine years. Their story had been one of great effort. They had obeyed the call of duty in the nation's hour of great peril and need, and the nation owed them an everlasting debt.

HM Queen Elizabeth inspecting members of the Women's Land Army
at Buckingham Palace, in October 1950.

Later that afternoon, the five-hundred WLA members who had been inspected by the Queen attended the first harvest thanksgiving service to be held in St Paul's Cathedral for fifty years.

A copy of Her Majesty's speech appeared in the final number of *Land Army News*, as did a message from the Minister of Agriculture. The following year, when the King invested Lady Denman with the Grand Cross of the British Empire, he said, 'We always thought that the Land Girls were not well treated.'

Corn sowing, 1943.
WLA volunteer, Jean Young (later Mrs Jean Procter), checking machine.
'The machine was pulled by a tractor. Occasionally the spouts where the seed came
down became clogged, and one had to stop and empty them, or there were bare patches
in spring - and then you were in trouble!'

11

Custodians of a Rural Heritage

Over 200,000 girls have served for longer or shorter periods in the Land Army. I wonder will any two former Land Army members ever meet, discover their shared past and still feel themselves strangers. I think not. I think the country will come alive for them again as they talk. I think that in a very few minutes they will be back in the old days. In their old jobs. I think past and present will quickly be bridged by just three words - Do you remember? - Do you remember?

Inez Jenkins, CBE (WLA Chief Administrator, 1945-8)

Country living did not, of course, impress everyone. Many were the farmers' daughters whose departure from the farms had been prevented only by the war, and who now wanted to join those women whose sole connection with agriculture was the food they ate! Many disbanded Land Girls, returning to urban living, and women leaving the farms for the first time, were to join (or rejoin) the National Union of Townswomen's Guilds (NUTG), whose sharper political voice was more to their liking than that of the rural NFWI. They found in the Guild a message similar to that of the WIs, but one uncomplicated by the traditional rural hierarchy.

The Guild was founded in 1929, after Margery Corbett Ashby had heard a leading suffragist, Millicent Fawcett, exhorting women to 'go forward and educate the new citizens'. A joint Committee representing both the Guild and the WI continued for some years after the formation of the NUTG. If an application was received from a village whose population exceeded the Institute's maximum size, or came from a small town Guild, the Committee would confer and decide which of the two should enrol the new member. There are no prizes for guessing that Lady Denman had been involved in setting up the NUTGs! The link was Mrs Eva Hubback, Parliamentary Secretary of the National Union of Women's Suffrage Societies, and a mutual friend, not only of Mrs Corbett Ashby, but also of Lady Denman. Mrs Hubback had persuaded Lady Denman to organise a fund-raising party at Balcombe Place in order to help collect the £15,000 they needed to start up Townswomen's Guilds all over the country.

During the war, the Guilds were to prove of great assistance to the Government, and were used to help promote a change in women's kitchen habits in accordance with rationing. Caroline Merz, in her history of the Townswomen's Guilds, written in the movement's diamond jubilee year, observed:

> As well as individual Guild enterprises, the NUTG as a whole co-operated directly with various Ministries, including the Ministry of Food under Lord Woolton . . . Many Guilds took to growing vegetables in a big way: Hounslow, for instance, got an allotment in their local park and learned the hard way how to cultivate potatoes, sprouts, turnips, spinach and many other vegetables. Many other Townswomen joined the Women's Land Army which, in several parts of the country, employed part-time seasonal workers. Their 'holidays' were spent in often far from romantic settings helping with the harvest, tending to animals, and, of course, digging.

While plans for post-war reconstruction were being made, the surviving members of the Women's Farm and Garden Association, denied a role in wartime, used their resources to offer advice to women seeking a career in agriculture or horticulture. The Council of the WFGA had been kept active by Dr Kate Barratt (Principal of Swanley College), and in 1943 a committee prepared a report on the prospects of careers for women in the various branches of agriculture. Other reports followed, concerning women's conditions of work and pay, the prospects for smallholders, and developments in public parks and botanic gardens. Advertisements, inviting women to attend interviews for post-war employment and training, appeared in *The Land Girl* during 1945. In the February of that year, Hertfordshire members of the WFGA forwarded a Resolution to WLA officials to the effect that 'WLA headquarters should notify WLA members individually of the WFGA's ability to give professional help and advice to those who wish to continue on the land after the war.'

The Association regained possession of Courtauld House in 1945, and work started on repairing the bomb damage. Initial costs were borne by the War Damage Commission, but dry rot had set in, and the Association was to be saddled with an enormous debt that continued to dog it for the next fifteen years. By 1947, the new Clubhouse was fully operational, with Miss G. Forster appointed as Warden. In the same year, Miss Vanderpant retired as Organising Secretary, to be succeeded two years later by Miss Barbara Crosland, who held the post for the next twelve years. In 1948, Dr Kate Barratt took office as Treasurer.

The Fiftieth anniversary of the Association fell in 1949, and was marked by a visit to Courtauld House by the Queen. That same year, the old standing committees were finally disbanded, and a single Council of Management formed, specific interests being dealt with by short-term committees - a system that has been retained, virtually unchanged, until the present day. In 1952, the Association once more had stands at the Royal Show and the Chelsea Flower Show. In 1953, when Cold War tensions made peace appear precarious, a small *ad hoc* committee was even formed to consider recreating the disbanded Women's Land Army.

The committee's findings were not, however, needed. Nor, it seemed, was the WFGA. By 1964 its membership stood at an all-time low of seven hundred and fifty. Indeed, so grave was the financial position that Courtauld House had to be sold to raise capital, and there was a strong lobby in favour of winding up the Association and donating its assets to some organisation with similar aims. That this did not happen owes much to the fact that no similar organisation existed. Members instead had a re-think, and realised that they had a duty to fight for the future of women land workers who, under different conditions, might once more need the help of a strong central organisation. According to its historian,

> The Association entered a period in which few innovative schemes were launched, membership was rapidly declining, the Employment Bureau was virtually inoperative, and, except in one or two areas, regional meetings could no longer be sustained because of low membership and lack of interest. The main pre-occupation of Council was to preserve the assets intact and to live within the income generated by them, until such time as a genuine need for the old pioneering spirit of the Association could be identified. In the meantime, members received regular newsletters, stands were taken at some shows, and fairly well-attended conferences were held once or twice a year in different parts of the country. A steady flow of some 2,000 enquiries per year on careers, jobs, etc. came into the office and were dealt with, and these indeed, justified the continuing existence of the Association since they came in for years after an active programme of careers advice had been discontinued.

The Association was to make one more stand for women land workers before settling down to its present role as an information and referral agency. In 1969, Studley Agriculture and Horticulture College for Women was closed by the Department of Education and Science. Single-sex colleges were no longer approved of by the Government and Studley was very expensive to run. The WFGA unsuccessfully joined with other interested organisations in fighting for the College's reprieve. The building was eventually sold to British Leyland for use as a venue for weekend conferences. The Studley Guild, which began life in 1900 as the Guild of the Daughters of Ceres, still keeps former students and staff in touch.

Links with the ever-strengthening Associated Country Women of the World (ACWW), and a place on European Community committees, whose decisions affect women in agriculture, brings the WFGA into a modern context. In 1989 it hosted the annual meeting of the Women's Committee of the Comité des Organisations Professionnelles Agricoles (COPA), at the Royal Agricultural College at Cirencester. A European Committee, which usually holds its meetings in Brussels,

COPA is involved with legislation affecting the equality of working conditions for farmers' wives, and looking for a system of social protection that will place them on an equal footing with others employed on the farm.

'What of the future?' the WFGA asks in its latest recruitment leaflet:

> Inevitably this will be affected by the state of British agriculture in general, and this is facing considerable changes and re-adjustments. Women working on the land will still need a strong central organisation to keep a watching brief on their particular problems, but perhaps there may be more need for the Association to look beyond the shores of this country and consider ways of helping the food-producing women of the Third World.

There can be no doubt that the formidable ladies who founded the Association in 1899 would be heartened, and reassured, to know that the WFGA today shows no signs of a shortage of innovative ideas or any lack of pioneering spirit. It has recently initiated a training scheme for women over twenty-five who wish to return to work in British agriculture. The Association has recently had to cease its connection with the ACWW, because of a continual stretching of WFGA funds; but the ACWW itself has grown into the largest international organisation of rural women, with nine million members in more than seventy countries throughout the world.

The Women's Institutes have flourished too, although unlike the WFGA, they are concerned more with country living than with professional employment in agriculture or horticulture. Since the activities of the WIs and of the WLA were necessarily of a similar nature, there was much common ground. It would, however, be a mistake to confuse the two memberships.

During the early years of the Second World War, there had been some clashes in the villages about the way in which the WI members were given authority over the allocation of farm labour. It did in fact make sense for the existing structure of the Institutes to undertake this responsibility, and, under the unifying banner of war, peace was generally maintained. Vita Sackville-West expressed it thus:

> Let us recognise that [the Land Girl] usually belongs to a different class of birth and upbringing, and also (which is quite as significant) to a different generation . . . It is perhaps a little unfair to set every well-meaning Rep. down as 'Lady Blimp', but let us at least recognise that some divergence of point of view must inevitably arise between the staid squire-archy of middle-age and gay wild youth out for all the fun it can get.

Certainly most of the senior staff in the Land Army were drawn from Lady Denman's WIs, and so were unlikely to have signed up as full-time 'land fodder' themselves! Though weekend jaunts, or four weeks on a neighbouring farm, were acceptable towards the end of the war, prejudice against land work still existed among country women of a certain social status, who regarded it as *lowering*. One young woman, who went on to become a leader in the NFWI, ran away from home to join the second WLA. She was brought back swiftly by her naval officer father, who would rather she did anything than go on the land! Many land workers were later to join the Institutes, but although throughout the war they were encouraged to do so, there was no real pull while they were still rookie Land Girls.

Although a correspondent in the *Farmer and Stock-Breeder* described a typical winter's evening entertainment as 'watching our tired husbands having a doze by the fire while we darn socks and wish the wireless battery had not given out!' the hoped-for influx of young women flocking to join the WIs after 1945 failed to materalise. The difficulty in attracting new and younger members to the Institutes was much the same then as it is now. The demands of farming, and bringing up a family, leave only a limited time for clubs or other formal gatherings, and baby sitters are a rare breed in some rural areas. Often it is not until many country women reach middle-age that they find time for these activities.

If the basis of the WIs was Adelaide Hoodless's message of 'home-maker and citizen builder' it was never her intention to free women from that role! The generation of women who served in the Land Army, and who were then to make their future as farmers' wives had fewer, and therefore easier choices. Cicely McCall, writing in 1942, in her book, *Women's Institutes*, scanned the Scott Report for recommendations of 'revivification of country areas', and commented:

> The test time for the Institutes is going to come after the war. Tired elderly members will have to make room for demobilised younger members, not to be replaced by them but to work alongside them. We shall want the wider experience and different outlook of the younger members as well as the maturer wisdom of older women if peacetime villages are to be living units, not crumbling relics. Democracy has been well-taught and practised in Institutes, and when peace comes there will be 300,000 women ready to say loudly and clearly that since country people are 'custodians of a heritage' that heritage must be living, not embalmed.

It is not so simple any more. Women today are less responsive to society's emotional blackmail to keep them in line, while farming is being relieved of its traditional responsibility as custodian of the rural heritage. Young women brought up on isolated farms are now open to influences and ideals far beyond those of the 1940s. In some of the new political movements, and in the growing importance of environmental issues to all parties, there is the beginning of compromise; although some interpretations of 'green' thinking, heavily politicised as it is, can create conflict for women in the role of farmer, or farmer's wife. The WI movement has, from its inception, campaigned for such things as clean water, food hygiene, and healthy living. It has yet to be seen whether these, now fashionable, issues will boost the WIs membership, and if it still has the authority to act as a forum in such matters.

Lady Denman saw the post-war period as a time for the WIs to consolidate, and to fight the planners, who, as she observed, 'thought that the ordinary small village has no future'. However, at the first full peace-time Annual General Meeting of the WI, in May 1946, she made it clear that she was no longer able to be in charge of such battles, and resigned as Chairman of the National Federation. That same year saw the completion of plans for an Institute College, to be known as Denman College, which was duly opened, at Marcham Park, in September 1948. For those who had followed Lady Denman through nearly thirty years it was difficult to conceive of the National Federation without her, and it is a tribute to the leadership of this remarkable woman that the movement was by then robust enough to survive on its own merits, rather than on those of a single individual.

Suffering from bouts of ill-health, Lady Denman shed several of her other responsibilities at the same time. Her old friend, Nellie Grant, was to visit Balcombe when she could, and Margaret Pyke, former Editor of *The Land Girl*, continued to live there. While often appearing austere, to those who met her for the first time, the warmth and generosity Lady Denman extended to those she loved was cherished by the recipients. She died on the 2 June 1954, following an operation. Her influence is inestimable, and women today still have reason to be grateful to her for championing the cause both of farm and country women.

Part II

What happened to the women who fed a nation at war? Did they shrug their shoulders when it was all over, and return home? Were the Department Stores bursting with ex-WLA girls returning to their counters, and had the newly-acquired urge to plant each season's crop vanished without a trace? It surely cannot be nostalgia alone that makes hundreds of former Land Army and Timber Corps members attend National Reunions, or organise enthusiastic and rousing get-togethers, forty years after the second Women's Land Army was disbanded.

The remaining women land workers kept working on Britain's farms for nearly five years after the war ended. The Timber Corps was wound up on 31 August 1946, but the WLA machinery kept turning. In March 1947, *The Land Girl* was succeeded by *Land Army News*, which kept its readers in touch with each other and a reduced administrative staff until November 1950. People had to eat, and the women acknowledged their moral responsibility to plant the crops in the spring of 1946. One of the few differences in post-war working conditions was the fact that the womens' services were now entirely voluntary. This meant a lower percentage of failure, and fewer drop outs. By no means all WLA placings had proved successful. One farmer's wife spoke with resignation of her experience:

We only had two Land Girls. One spent most of her time in the lavatory reading love letters, and the second got ill the day after she arrived. I had to nurse her for a month, and do her work on top of everything else.

Motivation in the shape of war had gone, to be replaced by another. The needs of the country were, from 1945 onwards, to be intensified by the thousands of returning servicemen putting further strain on home food production. The continuation of rationing convinced those anxious to leave the farms that the success of the next few harvests was still vital. The women who remained on the farms became aware of the subtle changes taking place in agriculture, of which the most important and most dramatic was mechanisation. Herman Simper, in his *Arable Machinery*, described the change:

> The reaper, the binder, the threshing drum and straw pitcher were living on numbered days... The harvest of 1946 was to be a grim and muddy affair in the main cereal areas of Eastern England... Farmers, with ground-driven binders, and those who were a little old fashioned with their tackle, struggled for two months and more in quagmire conditions. Those who had progressed to a power-driven binder fared better. They were not to be found prone on their backs wrapping sacks round the giant driving wheel mounted amidships on the old binders. Like everybody else, the lucky few who had a combine could only snatch at the odd few hours of sunshine that came but what they reaped was theirs for the keeping.

The number of horses used in agriculture had, by 1914, already declined from their peak of 1.1 million. By 1958, horses were no longer a routine part of the agricultural census, and a decade later were not recorded at all. The decline of horse power, and rapid mechanisation, shadowed the reduction in the labour force. Although the number of agricultural workers had risen during the war above the pre-1938 low of 700,000, it was to decline rapidly thereafter, reaching less than 300,000 by the end of the 1980s. After 1945, men slowly returned to the farms, and, as they did so, women had to accept that they were once more in competition for jobs. Prejudice in favour of male labour re-established itself, even though many women were now as well trained as men.

Young women, whom the war had freed from parental restraint and financial dependence, realised that with the peace they would be expected to return home as if nothing had happened. Most, indeed, were happy to regard their Land Army days as nothing more than an interlude in their lives, and to return gratefully to suburbia. A core of dedicated women, however, who had become hooked on farming, did not wish to leave at all. For some of these the solution was obvious - and they duly married their bosses, or their bosses' sons! This might also have solved the immediate problem of employment: once married, and a wife, she would go some way towards relieving any shortage of labour on the farm!

Former members of the WLA who write or who speak of their decision to marry farmers, rarely complain that they had no idea what they were letting themselves in for! Any volunteer who remained on the land as a wife did so with her eyes open - which is more than can be said for many at the start of their agricultural careers!

One member wrote:

> The farmer was a widower. I lived in the farmhouse with him and his housekeeper. The farmer's son was in the Dorset Yeomanry, and had been called up before the outbreak of the war, and was away in the army. Of course I met him when he came home on leave, and, like the classic fairy tale, I married the farmer's son in 1946. We are still in Ludwell, and have raised a family of two girls and one boy, all of whom are now married. My son has now moved into the farmhouse with his wife and two small boys, whilst we live in a cottage close by.

An ex-WLA woman, who left London to work on the land, wrote:

> Another Land Army girl and I [played] darts in the local pub. It was there that I met my husband. He worked for Bulmers, on the Nursery Farm, growing cider apple trees. Now I started learning about a different type of farming. Although I enjoyed real farming, the growing of young apple trees and watching them blossom was special to me, and it made a lot of difference to my life, especially when Frank and I got married. Then my husband was made manager of the Nursery Farm at Hampton Bishop, near Hereford. I knew I could be of some use to him. We would talk about his work together. Soon I was able to work on the farm. I had fulfilled my dream: farming, living near Hereford, and having a lovely husband, and four children. Now we have four grandchildren. My husband retired, having planted over a million cider apple trees. I would not change my life to go back to London.

Not all women who wished to stay on the land viewed marriage as the only course; and many set about job hunting. In November 1950, the Ministry of Agriculture produced a pamphlet entitled 'To Members of the WLA staying on the Land', although the girls could have worked out much of the advice for themselves, or obtained it from the WFGA. To have been attracted by membership of the WLA, and to have been a successful member, women usually possessed (or acquired) either an unconventional nature, or a spirited sense of independence. For those willing to reject security in favour of adventure, the Society for the Overseas Settlement of British Women had something to offer. Its General Secretary, Ellen Cumber, informed readers of the *Land Army News*:

> If at any time you are thinking of taking up work in some part of the British Commonwealth we shall be glad to help and advise you ... there is a real welcome in almost every part of the Commonwealth for adaptable and hard working women. Australia and New Zealand offer £10 fares to British immigrants, and in Canada a 'Settlement Service' has been set up to place British men and women in employment. The SOSBW can supply you with full details of these schemes on application.

Farmers in the Dominions, however, had still to be converted to the idea that women could be valuable on a farm.

The remaining link, which former members of the WLA and those still in service in 1950, had in common, was the WLA Benevolent Fund. This brought much comfort to members who had fallen on hard times, due to illness or misfortune, and it had guided the steps of those who discovered that the 'Cinderella service' would not bestow upon its members that same good fortune enjoyed by the fairytale Cinders. Real hardship existed for many Land Army girls even if, for some, the Fund itself often seemed to be the last official proof that there ever had been a Land Army at all. There remained, however, thousands of women throughout the British Isles, Europe, and the Commonwealth, who never forgot their Land Army experiences, and who wished in some way to relive the years during which they had answered the nation's call, as well as the contribution they had made to maintaining the country's wartime food supplies. For most, the WLA days represented their youth and freedom. They needed something new, which at the same time made cele-

WLA Group for Romiley, Cheshire, and the surrounding villages, 1942.
Jean Young *(far left, seated),* was later, as Mrs Jean Procter, to organise
the first WLA reunion in 1964.

bration of the past. In 1964, quite by accident, that 'something' was born. A former WLA member, Mrs Jean Procter, happened to meet an ex-WLA colleague. They talked of their years as Land Girls, and as Mrs Procter knew the whereabouts of one or two others, she felt that they should all get together for tea at her home.

'News,' she recalls wryly, 'travels fast; it somehow got out that it was a National reunion, and I had letters from women all over the country asking me if they could come too. There were even letters saying that coach loads were preparing to come along. The doorbell never stopped ringing, and the mail came in bundles and bags.'

This 'little tea party' was an overwhelming success. On the day, some ninety people squeezed into her home at Marple, in Cheshire. Fortunately, the late autumn day was fine, and the reunion was able to spill out into the garden! The press turned out in force, and national newspapers were to carry photographs of the event. From that moment there was no possibility of stemming the tide of other ex-Land Girls who wanted the same opportunity of reliving their days on the land. Mrs Procter wrote to every county newspaper for which she could find an address, asking to be put in touch with any woman interested in attending a National Reunion. Barbara Ellis, who helped Mrs Procter organise that first Land Army reunion, recalls:

> It took us over two years to gather names and addresses of Land Girls, as there seemed to be no records at all. To crown it all, we had to issue all the tickets . . . ourselves, and there was a postal strike before we had finished.

From the replies she received Mrs Procter picked out 'links' for different areas, and made up a small news-sheet on a very old, hand-turned, Gestetner.

Support was such that, in January 1968, Mrs Procter signed a contract to hire the Royal Albert Hall for a National WLA Reunion. There was nearly a year to sort out the applications, and to organise the event. This was just as well, for it proved a major undertaking. Every applicant was asked to supply as many details as possible, in order that county groups might be kept together. Similarly, women who had lived in the same hostel, or worked on the same farm, were grouped together. The triumphant success of that day, 1 February 1969, is best described by Mrs Procter herself:

> Five thousand ex-WLA [members] packed the Royal Albert Hall for the most fantastic Reunion of all time, I would think. There were people all over the Hall finding themselves sitting next to friends they had not seen for years. It was a most moving and emotional sight, and one I will never forget. It made all the sleepless nights, and the hard never-ending slog to accomplish this wonderful day, worthwhile. The Lord Mayor of London was there, as well as the Lord Mayor of Westminster. Both having readily accepted the invitation I had sent. The Manager of the Royal Albert Hall, and all the staff, were so very helpful, and it all went with swing.

Nor was it only women from the Second World War who had been reunited. Also present were one hundred and forty-three former WLA members from the First

World War. As a result of their efforts, both Barbara Ellis and Mrs Procter were to be invited to the Woman of the Year luncheon held in London later that year. But if Mrs Procter imagined that this perfect day was to be a unique occasion, she was mistaken. In poured the letters again, and this time there was nothing for it - a Reunion Society was formed, with a subscription of 6s. 6d. a year, and the members receiving regular news-sheets. Independent county groups were created, with Societies even being formed in Canada, Australia, and New Zealand. Eight more National Reunions were to follow, three at the Royal Albert Hall. In 1988 The Queen Mother attended one held at the Grand Hotel in Birmingham. As the Chairman, Mrs Procter, wrote afterwards:

HM Queen Elizabeth, The Queen Mother.
As Queen Elizabeth, during the Second World War, The Queen Mother was Patron of both the WLA and its Benevolent Fund. She was here attending the 7th National WLA and WTC Reunion, held at the Grand Hotel in Birmingham, on 30 April 1988.

Her Majesty captivated all our hearts with her friendliness and charm. She never seems to stop smiling and shows so much genuine interest in everyone and everything, and gives the impression that they are important to her at that time. I am sure that it was a day that we will never forget, and anyone who came near to her will have felt a surge of affection and joy which will be forever etched on the mind.

In her speech, the Queen Mother recalled her amazement at meeting women with peacetime occupations as varied as dressmaker, shoe shop assistant, pools clerk for Littlewoods, and typist for the railways, who were miraculously transformed into threshing gangs, fruit farming, pig farming, market gardening, pest control officers, or general farmers.

Over the years the county groups have strengthened - some, like Suffolk, Lincolnshire, and Norfolk, becoming independent from the British WLA Society. In Norfolk there have been two major reunions, both held at the Gressenhall Rural Life Museum near Dereham. Here, hundreds of members have donned their wartime uniform, and taken part again in working demonstrations of farm and forestry work, 1940s style!

In the small Norfolk village of Heydon, during the long hot summer of 1976, there were other preparations recalling Land Army days, when Anglia Television started filming a new comedy series, 'Backs to the Land', intended as a tribute to the Land Girls. When shown, it received, naturally enough, a mixed reaction. As Sheila Jenner, *British Farmer & Stockbreeder's* Farmer's Home Editor, commented:

The series is giving real life ex-land girls a rueful laugh as they watch the exploits of their TV counterparts . . . though it is a pity about that suggestive title recalling the most unsubtle of the Land Army jokes. Nice to see the girls getting some recognition though, and even a telly comedy makes it easier to answer the question: 'What did you do in the war, granny?

Part III

In the years since 1950, the role of women who work on the land has not been as well-investigated as it might have been. In 1980, however, the WFGA commissioned a survey on *The Role of Women in British Agriculture*, conducted by Dr Ruth Gasson. Some of those who took part had been introduced to farm life through the WLA. Dr Gasson wrote:

I was surprised to find that of 13 women on dairy farms, 12 were never expected to do the milking; most claimed that they had never been taught. At first I took this to be a blatant example of male chauvinism. Further probing suggested that women can be chauvinists too. Several admitted they had taken good care not to learn milking. One woman had warned her daughter never to let anyone teach her how to dress a chicken, drive a tractor, or milk a cow.

The Report found that women accounted for a little over a quarter of the farm labour force, and commented, 'Considering the magnitude of their contribution, surprisingly little is known about these women and the work they do'.

The final collection of data - put together with the help of Wye College, the Agricultural Training Board, and *Farmers Weekly* - had to wait until 1989 for a sequel; but hidden away towards the end of the first Survey is a paragraph that will appeal to many women, on the land or not:

Women strive to achieve a double standard. Besides the traditional feminine achievements of domestic comfort, and satisfying family relationships, they are exhorted to extend themselves and make careers outside the home. If they try to compete with men in their chosen occupation, they face discrimination from the men whose position is threatened. As women, they are disapproved of if they attempt to do less than the full-time housewife. If they strive too hard for both goals they become overworked and their physical or mental health may suffer. If, as most inevitably do, they fail to achieve high standards simultaneously in home-making and a career, they feel guilty. On top of this the farm woman has to cope with problems of rural isolation, bad weather, peaks of labour demand, farm crises, her husband's long and unpredictable hours, fluctuating farm income, and a business which is run from home.

While Dr Gasson was conducting her survey, a group of Kent farmers' wives were together creating the newest of the British farm womens' organisations - The Women's Farming Union (WFU). This is unique in its intent, having an unashamedly high commercial profile and a practical modern image, with very definite views about linking the producer with the consumer.

The Women's Farming Union started in the apple-growing areas of England, shortly after Britain's entry into the EEC when there were worries that British apples were not faring well in the face of increased competition. The Apple Campaign established the WFU as a nationwide organisation acutely aware of what membership of the European Community actually means to British farmers. The Union has already expanded into Scotland and Wales, and, while most of its members are based in the countryside, membership is open to anyone interested in rural affairs, including NUTG women, who take part in the Union's shopping surveys. In association with the Agricultural Training Board, the WFU has produced a leaflet, *Training for Women*, and it encourages employment for women in agriculture and horticulture. One member of the Union's Central Executive Council, Mrs Sarah Ward, set out their objectives thus:

Its purpose is a particularly appropriate one for women, whose traditional role has been to take farm produce to market, and present it to the buyer. At a time when the great bulk of the population is becoming ever more remote from food production this role is of supreme importance to agriculture. The WFU is the only agricultural organisation to dedicate itself to communication between the farmer and the customer.

Mrs Ward also reminded the 1989 meeting of COPA's Women's Committee:

How many people realise, for example, what the members of my audience here will be well-aware of, that eighty per cent of the world's agricultural work is done by women? That when we import Brazilian coffee, cocoa, or Ceylon tea, to satisfy our insatiable need for caffeine, we are not only importing the fertility of the soil from poorer countries but exploiting peasant female labour as well. Are those who complain that the Common Agriculture Policy is expensive willing for European agricultural labour to revert to the peasant conditions which we shared with the third world until the advent of mechanisation in the last century?

Baroness Trumpington, later Minister of State at the Ministry of Agriculture, who joined the Land Army in 1939, seen here with the Rt. Hon. David Lloyd George, on whose estate at Churt, in Surrey, she worked for two years.

In October 1989, a former Land Girl was on hand to offer official recognition of the WFUs Tenth anniversary. Baroness Trumpington (Jean Alys Barker), Minister of State at the Ministry of Agriculture, had joined the WLA in 1939, and worked for two years on David Lloyd George's estate at Churt in Surrey. Fifty years later she was able to congratulate the Union on behalf of the Government, and to pass on a message from the Prime Minister:

> Women - both as farmers and as paid, or even unpaid, workers - have always played a major role in our farming communities. The formation of the WFU reflects the need for more effective marketing of British produce, and the WFU has played a major role, as a catalyst, in creating better links between farmers and growers and their customers.

British farming has changed out of all recognition since those Land Army days. No-one today is asked to pull acres of sugar beet by hand, or to squat in four inches of mud in a bleak December tugging hopelessly at unyielding udders! The urgent requirements of wartime agriculture, and the war itself, hastened scientific advances. This, combined with the longer-term government support provided by the Agriculture Act, 1947, produced unexpected results. The ensuing prosperity, and unequalled efficiency, reached its fruition in the 1960s. By the time she entered the European Economic Community, in 1973, Britain and most of Europe had enough to eat. Such agricultural success had a price: news of food mountains and wine lakes began to undermine the old wartime image of an efficient industry providing food for a hungry nation.

The provision of plentiful and cheap food in Britain is now almost regarded as a right, its easy distribution and processing in convenience form has become part of the process of liberating women from chores which their grandmothers took in their stride, but then, for most of our grandmothers, there was no other work.

That a woman's place in agriculture has not been so strongly established as in other areas, may be from choice. Farming deals with living things; animals and crops bring unpredictable calls for attention, and for those who practise it, it becomes a way of life not simply a business. Women no longer, at least, have to marry to enter farming! Those with degrees in agriculture have been able to join international companies as researchers or sales representatives, and there are numerous female lecturers in agriculture-related subjects at colleges and universities. An increasing proportion of veterinary students are female, and there are even freelance women shepherds.

As with all advances there is a reckoning, and now, as we enter the 1990s the price is evident in terms of a realisation of the finite resources of the planet. In a predominantly urban society British women are now further removed from the realities of agriculture than were either of the generations who met the demands of the two World Wars. Surely such unromantic appeals to patriotism as were made in 1914 and 1939 would today be totally resistable? Yet, for millions of farm women world-wide, women's role on the land - whether in war or peace-time - continues to inspire, frustrate, and absorb. From the First World War, when women first rallied in support of home agriculture, and through the gruelling years of the Second World War, that role, until recently, has barely changed. However, the world *has* changed, and nowhere is that reflected better than in the birth of the Women's Farming Union, with its necessarily realistic message.

These islands are not now, thankfully, under siege, but farming's basis is once again being challenged, if not this time by war then by world events and domestic politics. Twice this century, governments have allowed domestic production to slip into recession. Twice, such expediency left this country on the brink of starvation. No-one now looks to war, or to a Third Land Army, to save this country; yet we cannot assume that such conditions might not recur, this time brought not by war but by our disregard for the global environment, and good husbandry.

Yet there is cause for hope. New generations can draw strength and inspiration from the pioneers of women's history - from the thousands of ordinary town women who joined British farmers in growing and nurturing the food required by two wartime populations - and from the experience of women, still in agriculture, who so reassuringly keep alive traditions of farming and of husbandry which are acutely important for our survival.

APPENDIX

TABLE 1
WOMEN'S LAND ARMY EMPLOYMENT RETURNS FOR ENGLAND

County	End Dec. 1939	End Dec. 1940	End Dec. 1941	End Dec. 1942	End Dec. 1943	End March 1945	Jan. 1947
Bedfordshire	24	55	140	492	990	992	663
Berkshire	103	214	534	1047	1209	1042	497
Buckinghamshire	54	108	403	1346	1836	1450	801
Huntingdonshire, Cambridgeshire, and Ely	63	113	428	828	1207	1075	541
Cheshire	100	259	570	1205	1436	1449	500
Cornwall	41	105	292	831	1411	1345	657
Cumberland and Westmorland	29	119	282	775	974	776	391
Derbyshire	30	78	158	331	533	521	193
Devonshire	114	164	391	1047	1708	1573	737
Dorset	103	-	319	712	881	-	367
Durham	5	-	156	568	1008	906	448
Essex	124	160	795	2509	3777	2971	1024
Gloucestershire	156	301	537	1125	1344	1183	568
Hampshire	138	421	866	1801	2248	1864	878
Herefordshire	47	88	255	509	650	629	360
Hertfordshire	65	138	445	1623	2162	1756	920
Isle of Wight	62	-	173	290	363	290	158

153

County	End Dec. 1939	End Dec. 1940	End Dec. 1941	End Dec. 1942	End Dec. 1943	End March 1945	Jan. 1947
Kent	262	475	1691	3126	3984	3773	1419
Lancashire	81	185	540	1174	1457	1258	316
Leicestershire and Rutland	120	172	627	1704	2145	1751	810
Holland	16 ⎱ 126		–	1308	536 ⎱		
Kesteven	126 ⎰				918 ⎰ 2004		897
Lindsey	217	118	291	586	740		
London and Middlesex	17	–	131	367	600	535	188
Monmouthshire	34	91	266	499	648	577	363
Norfolk	112	166	481	1087	1620	1414	582
Northamptonshire	93	165	543	1481	1834	1672	839
Northumberland	180	122	373	976	1386	1175	568
Nottinghamshire	29	104	452	1023	1299	1143	517
Oxfordshire	115	193	410	816	1090	930	589
Shropshire	103	155	372	861	1002	894	361
Somersetshire	163	238	454	1298	1794	1584	625
Staffordshire	65	131	268	676	777	721	400
Suffolk (East)	90	74	217	758	1138	960	442
Suffolk (West)	222	230	214	523	594	559	279
Surrey	121	271	781	1506	2361	2050	1226
Sussex (East)	153	239	771	1676	2022	1761	589
Sussex (West)	226	222	489	1229	1564	1473	694
Warwickshire	103	187	412	1351	1762	1425	799
Wiltshire	162	308	593	1113	1535	1312	453
Worcestershire	102	224	561	1392	1800	–	645
Yorkshire (East)	23	–	–	–	1091	896 ⎱	685
Yorkshire (North)	⎱ 89	219	1075	3776	4088	2908 ⎰	
Yorkshire (West)	⎰						897

TABLE 2
WOMEN'S LAND ARMY EMPLOYMENT RETURNS FOR WALES

County	End Dec. 1939	End Dec. 1940	End Dec. 1941	End Dec. 1942	End Dec. 1943	March 1945	Jan. 1947
North Wales	40	-	228	577	553	502	297
South Wales	30	150	294	628	360		
Breconshire and Radnorshire	-	-	101	283	304	256	269* (Including Montgomery)
Cardiganshire and Carmarthenshire	-	-	-	-	-	304	242
Denbighshire	53	67	136	-	575	533	251
Flintshire	10	67	104	359	602	509	323
Glamorganshire	49	-	-	-	698	695	410
Montgomeryshire	12	-	-	-	211	238	*
Pembrokeshire	8	-	-	-	406	375	145

General employment analysis, December 1943:
In private employment:
a) Milkers, or in milking and general farm work - 20,159
b) In other farm employment, not including milking - 12,521
c) Horticultural employment - 10,817
d) In other jobs - 1,674

Employed by War Agricultural Executive Committees: 26,374
Timber Corps: 4,339 (In March 1945 this stood at 2,677)

On 30 March 1945, the number of volunteers in employment was approximately 60,950
On 18 January 1947, the total number of volunteers in employment was 26,823

TABLE 3
SCOTTISH WOMEN'S LAND ARMY EMPLOYMENT RETURNS
(NOVEMBER 1943)

County	Total	County	Total
Aberdeen	615	Lanark	582
Angus	241	Midlothian	545
Argyll	162	Moray	111
Ayr	1160	Nairn	60
Banff	95	Orkney	6
Berwick	322	Peebles	104
Bute	60	Perth	363
Caithness	29	Ross and Cromarty	188
Dumfries	330	Roxburgh	333
Dumbarton and Renfrew	449	Selkirk	56
East Lothian	390	Stirling and Clackmannan	269
Fife and Kinross	664	Sutherland	21
Inverness	139	West Lothian	117
Kincardine	113	Wigtown	210
Kirkcudbright	235	Zetland	7

156

BIBLIOGRAPHY

Baily, Leslie, *Scrapbook for the Twenties* (Frederick Muller, 1959)

Beddoe, Dierdre, *Discovering Women's History* (Pandora Press, 1983)

Boyce, D. George, *The Crisis of British Unionism* (The Historians' Press, 1987)

Calder, Angus, *The People's War Britain 1939-45* (Jonathan Cape, 1969)

Cooper, Jilly, *Animals in War* (William Heinemann, 1983)

Costello, John, *Love, Sex and War: Changing Values 1939-1945* (Pan Books, 1985)

Dakers, Caroline, *The Countryside at War 1914-18* (Constable, 1987)

Edlin, Herbert L., *Timber! Your Growing Investment* (HMSO, 1969)

Ernle, Lord (Rowland Prothero), *English Farming Past and Present* (Longmans, 1912)

Fawcett, Millicent Garrett, *Women's Suffrage, A Short History of a Great Movement* (The People's Books, 1912)

Gasson, Ruth, *The Role of Women in British Agriculture* (Women's Farm and Garden Association, 1980)

Goodenough, Simon, *Jam and Jerusalem* (William Collins, 1977)

Grieg, G.A., *Women's Work on the Land* (Jarrold & Sons, 1916)

Hockin, Olive, *Two Girls on the Land* (Edward Arnold, 1918)

Howard, Louise, and Hearnden, Beryl, (eds), *What Country Women Use* (Allen & Unwin, 1939)

Huxley, Gervas, *Lady Denman, GBE* (Chatto & Windus, 1961)

Jenkins, Inez, *The History of the Women's Institute Movement of England and Wales* (Oxford University Press, 1953)

Joad, C.E.M., *The Untutored Townsman's Invasion of the Country* (Faber & Faber, 1945)

Johnson, Walford, Whyman, John, Wykes, George, *A short economic and Social History of Twentieth Century Britain* (Allen & Unwin, 1967)

Joseph, S., *If Their Mothers Only Knew* (Faber & Faber, 1946)

Marks, H.F., (D.K. Britton, Ed.) *A Hundred Years of British Food & Farming, A Statistical Survey* (Taylor & Francis, 1989)

McCall, Cicely, *Women's Institutes* (William Collins, 1943)

McGuffie, Duncan, *Cabbages and Committees* (Faber & Faber, 1944)

Meiggs, Russell, *Home Timber Production (1939-1945)* (Crosby Lockwood, 1949)

Merz, Caroline, *After The Vote* (Norwich, Adprint Ltd., 1988)

Morrow, Elsa, 'Swanley College: 1889-1945' (Wye College)

Raeburn, Antonia, *Militant Suffragettes* (Michael Joseph, 1973)

Russell, Sir E. John, *English Farming* (William Collins, 1942)

Ryle, George, 'Beating About the Bush' (Forestry Commission, undated)

Sackville-West, V., *The Women's Land Army* (Michael Joseph, 1944)

Shewell-Cooper, W.E., *Land Girl, A Handbook for the Women's Land Army* (English Universities Press, undated)

Simper, Herman, *Farmers Guide to Arable Machinery* (Ipswich, Farming Press Ltd., 1977)

Stott, Mary, *Organization Woman* (William Heinemann, 1978)

Terraine, John, *Impacts of War 1914 & 1918* (Hutchinson, 1970)

Trevelyan, G.M., *English Social History* (The Reprint Society, 1948)

Wadge, D. Collett, *Women in Uniform* (Sampson Low, Marston & Co. Ltd., 1946)

Whitlock, Ralph, *A Short History of Farming in Britain* (John Baker Publishers Ltd., 1965)

Wolseley, Viscountess, *Women and the Land* (Chatto & Windus, 1916)

Other sources used:

Public Record Office: (MAF 59/1, 42/8, 59/21, 59/22)

Journal of the Board of Agriculture, Volume XXII (April 1915 - March 1916)

Journal of the Board of Agriculture, Volume XXIII (April 1916 - March 1917)

An Outline History of the Women's Farm & Garden Association (WFGA, 1987)

Farmers in a Changing World (Washington D.C., United States Department of Agriculture, 1940)

Meet the Members, A Record of the Timber Corps of the Women's Land Army (Bristol, Bennett Brothers Ltd.)

Index